THE COINS
OF
HAIDAR ALI AND TIPU SULTAN

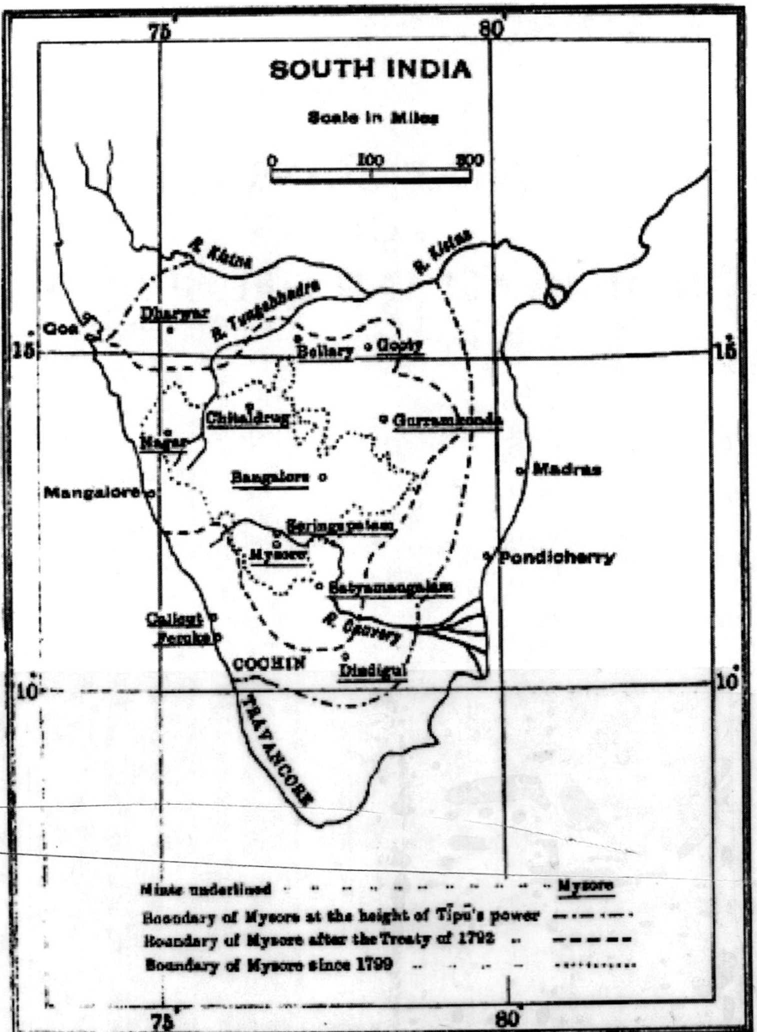

MINTS OF HAIDAR ALĪ AND TĪPŪ SULTĀN.

THE COINS
OF
HAIDAR ALI AND TIPU SULTAN

BY

J. R. HENDERSON, C.I.E., M.B., C.M. (EDIN.)

Formerly Superintendent, Madras Government Museum

GYAN

Published by

GYAN

Gyan Publishing House
5, Ansari Road
Daryaganj, New Delhi-110002
Phone: 011-47034999, 9811692060
E-mail: books@gyanbooks.com

Distribution Network
gyanbooks.com
India, USA, Canada, UK, Australia, France

ISBN : 978-81-212-3257-9 (PB)
First Published, 1921

2nd Impression 2020

Printed at: Gyan Press, Delhi.

The Coins of Haidar Ali and Tipu Sultan
Author: J. R. Henderson

THE COINS

OF

HAIDAR ALĪ AND TĪPŪ SULTĀN

BY

J. R. HENDERSON, C.I.E., M.B., C.M. (EDIN.)
Formerly Superintendent, Madras Government Museum.

MADRAS:
PRINTED BY THE SUPERINTENDENT, GOVERNMENT PRESS.

1921.

PREFACE.

THIS account of the coins of Haidar Alī and Tīpū Sultān is largely based on the collection of the Madras Government Museum, which, so far at least as the copper issues are concerned, is probably one of the most complete in existence. I have, however, also taken other sources into account, such as the works of previous writers, the large collections of the British Museum, London, and the Mysore Government Museum at Bangalore, as well as private collections. I regret that the notes which I took on the occasion of my visits to the two institutions just referred to are not as complete as I could have wished, and I have not been able to revisit these collections in recent years. The letter M following the number of a coin indicates that it is represented in the collection of the Madras Museum.

In cataloguing the somewhat complicated issues of Tīpū Sultān, I am convinced that, if confusion is to be avoided, the only safe course is to arrange the coins according to mints. In leaving the size of the coins to be inferred from the plates, and making comparatively little reference to their weight, I have perhaps laid myself open to adverse criticism ; but as most of the coins were roughly struck there are frequent variations in their size, and to some extent also in their weight. I have tried to indicate the chief variations in weight, without giving unnecessary details in regard to individual specimens.

In an attempt to indicate the relative scarcity or abundance of the different coins, I have perhaps ventured on an innovation in works of this kind. I have, however, attempted to do so on account of exceptional opportunities for forming such an opinion ; during a period of over quarter of a century many thousands of these coins, collected from all parts of Southern India, have passed through my hands.

All the coins entered in the catalogue without the name of an authority have been seen by myself, while some of those which are followed by the name of the writer who first recorded the coin, have not come under my personal examination. A good many are recorded for the first time, but it has not been thought necessary to particularize these.

In drawing up the short historical notes which accompany the catalogue, I have been struck by the fact that no adequate account of the lives of Haidar Alī and Tīpū Sulṭān has yet appeared. There must be unworked sources of information still available in Mysore, and I would express the hope that worthy biographies of these two remarkable men, written by one or more of their own countrymen, may yet appear.

In conclusion, while acknowledging my indebtedness to the various writers who have preceded me, I would specially mention the help I have received from the writings of Major R. P. Jackson and the Rev. Dr. G. P. Taylor, two of the latest authorities on the subject. Major Jackson's ist, based on his own collection, is the largest hitherto published, while the late Dr. Taylor, who applied his great knowledge of Indian Muhammadan coins to those of Tīpū Sultān, has furnished details in regard to the inscriptions and other matters on which I have freely drawn.

My thanks are due to Mr. G. F. Hill, Keeper of the Department of Coins and Medals, British Museum, and to Mr. J. Allan of the same Department, for assistance kindly rendered in connexion with the preparation of the plates, which have been printed at the University Press, Oxford.

MADRAS,
March, 1919.

J. R. HENDERSON.

CONTENTS.

THE COINS OF HAIDAR ALĪ AND TĪPŪ SULTĀN.

INTRODUCTION.

Many features of interest are presented by the coins of the two Muhammadan sovereigns who controlled the destinies of Mysore for the brief period of thirty-eight years,—Haidar Alī, the illiterate warrior, able in troublous and therefore propitious times to establish a kingdom by his forceful personality and military genius, and Tīpū Sultān, the son, who was unable to retain that kingdom. They are memorials of two remarkable men with whom Britain was frequently at war, issued at a time when the question of European supremacy in India was still in process of determination. But in addition to their historical associations and the light which they throw on the policy and even on the personal characteristics of the two rulers, there are other features which render the coins specially attractive to collectors. Many of them are still met with in considerable numbers, not only in the bazaars of nearly every Mysore village, but also over a considerable part of Southern India, while others again are of extreme rarity. The well-executed figure of an elephant, introduced by Haidar on some of the copper coins issued towards the close of his reign, and continued by Tīpū on all those struck in the same metal, forms a distinctive feature; many of the gold and silver pieces afford indisputable testimony to the decorative value of the Arabic script, and it may be doubted if any coin more attractive in this respect than Tīpū's double-rupee has ever been struck in India. For all these reasons it is not surprising that an extensive literature has sprung up on the subject, and no series of coins issued in South India and few in other parts of the country have been more often described or referred to.

The Mysore table-land during the first half of the eighteenth century consisted of several petty States ruled by more or less independent Poligars or Nāyaks, in addition to the larger and more important State of Mysore, then as now under the control of a Hindu Raja. To the north the chief powers were the Marāthās, a powerful Hindu confederation occupying what is now the southern part of the Bombay Presidency, with their capital at Poona, and the important Muhammadan State of Hyderabad, ruled by the Nizāms who controlled the greater part of Southern India and had practically set themselves free from Mughal sovereignty. The chief ruler in the south was the Nawāb of Arcot, who while nominally owing allegiance to the Nizām held sway over a considerable part of Southern India, including the district around Madras. Several Muhammadan chiefs, in what are now known as the Ceded Districts, viz., the Nawābs of Cuddapah, Kurnool, etc., and Morāri Rāo, the Marāthā ruler of Gooty, were also at this time feudatories of the Nizām's. Towards the middle of the eighteenth century, Mysore was subjected to constant invasions by the Marāthās, or by the Hyderabad forces, and sometimes by the two in conjunction.

Haidar Alī was born near Kolār in 1722, the son of a petty official of the Mysore State. After serving temporarily with the Nawāb of Arcot he took military service under Nanja Rāj, a minister of Mysore, who practically ruled the State although there was still a nominal Rājā; he gradually rose in favour and after achieving some distinction in campaigns during 1749 and 1751 was appointed military governor of Dindigul in 1755, the first important stage in his career. Promoted to the chief command against the Marāthās in 1759, who before long withdrew from Mysore territory, Haidar rose still further in authority and was enabled to supplant Nanja Rāj who had been virtual ruler for twenty years. Further trouble with the Marāthās arose two years later, but this was successfully overcome and he took possession of several small States, including Chitaldrūg, which adjoined Mysore, a period of annexation which in 1763 culminated in the capture of the important State of Bednūr, and this Haidar always regarded as having laid the foundation of his rise to greater power. The town of Bednūr, or Nagar as he termed it, became his capital and here for the first time he assumed the sovereign right of striking coins. He now succeeded in making terms with the Nizām, but was unable to appease the Marāthās, who only concluded peace when all the places previously taken from them had been restored and a large indemnity paid. In 1766 Malabar was taken by conquest and the Rājās of Cochin and Palghat capitulated. In the same year Chikka Krishna Rājā, the nominal ruler of Mysore, died, and although his son succeeded him, Haidar assumed entire control of the State.

In 1767 the Marāthās again invaded Mysore, and in the same year the British in alliance with the Nizām's forces took the field in what is known as the First Mysore War. During this campaign, in which Haidar showed great military ability, he was able in April 1769 to dictate terms to the British, practically at the very gates of Madras. Further trouble arose with the Marāthās in 1772, with disastrous results, and once more he was forced to conclude a treaty restoring territory and to pay a large monetary compensation. About this time the nominal Rājā of Mysore was strangled, and as his brother who succeeded him died soon after without an heir, a child was selected by Haidar as a representative, at any rate in name, of the ruling family. In 1773 Coorg was captured, a mountainous province adjoining Malabar, and the latter district which had broken out into revolt was soon after forced to submit. Three years later several of the smaller States bordering on Mysore, including Bellary and Gooty were recaptured, and owing to the defeat of the combined armies of the Marāthās and the Nizām, with whom he was once more at war, he was able to take possession of all the Marāthā territory south of the River Kistna and also of the Cuddapah district.

The year 1780 saw the commencement of the Second Mysore War, in which Haidar Alī with promised assistance from his former foes, the Marāthās and the Nizām, which, however, never matured, and the active co-operation of the French then at war with England, formed a very powerful combination against the British forces in India. In that year he advanced with a large army towards the east coast and actually arrived within a few miles of Madras, but after some initial success he was eventually defeated by Sir Eyre Coote at Porto Novo in July 1781, and later at Arni. Haidar died in camp near Chittoor in the North Arcot district, while his army was returning to Mysore, on 7th December 1782, or the first day of the *Hijri* year 1197. His body was taken to Seringapatam and buried there in state.

Haidar Alī owed his success to great natural ability, and more particularly to ability in war which often reached the heights of genius. He was wholly illiterate and unable either to read or to write, his signature never getting beyond the stage of the initial letter of his name, which is so familiar on his own gold coins and on the gold and silver coins of his son. He is said to have treated his subjects fairly, to have administered justice impartially and to have encouraged the arts of peace; but on the other hand he was frequently guilty of the grossest cruelty. Bowring (*Haidar Alī and Tipū Sultān, Rulers of India*, p. 113) thus refers to him:—"Whatever defects may be justly attributed to Haidar as a ruler, or in his private life, he was a bold, an original, and an enterprising commander, skilful in tactics and fertile in resources, full of energy, and never desponding in defeat. Notwithstanding the severity of his internal rule, and the terror which he inspired, his name is always mentioned in Mysore with respect, if not with admiration. While the cruelties which he sometimes practised are forgotten, his prowess and success have an abiding place in the memory of the people."

Tīpū Sultān who was born at Devanhalli, Mysore State, in 1753, commenced his reign while engaged in war with the British and it may be added terminated it in like manner seventeen years later. The Second Mysore War ended early in 1784, one of the contributing causes being the conclusion of peace between France and England in the previous year; the peace conditions with Tīpū included the restitution of prisoners on both sides and the restoration of all conquered territory. In 1783 Bednūr or Nagar, which had been taken by General Matthews in January, was recaptured by Tīpū three months later, and he was enthroned here with great ceremony on the 4th of May, a day recorded on many of his gold and silver coins, and by a strange coincidence also the anniversary of his death. About this time great cruelties were perpetrated by Tīpū on the west coast and in Coorg, where large numbers of Hindus and Christians were forcibly converted to Islām. Throughout his reign he showed intense zeal in the propagation of his religion, coupled with a great deal of narrow-minded bigotry, in these respects reversing the general policy of his father who always exhibited toleration in religious matters.

In 1786 the combined forces of the Marāthās and the Nizām declared war, and peace was only concluded in the following year on Tīpū restoring a number of forts which he had previously captured and paying a considerable indemnity. On his return to Seringapatam which was now the capital, he gave orders for the demolition of the old town of Mysore, in order to destroy the chief evidence of the deposed Hindu Rājās, and the new fort Nazarbār was erected in its immediate vicinity. In 1788 he visited Calicut, and for reasons similar to those which actuated him in the destruction of Mysore, arranged for the demolition of the capital of Malabar and the transfer of his government from Calicut to Feroke. During this period, while his power was at its zenith, he assumed the title of Bādshāh or King and dispatched ambassadors to Constantinople and Paris, chiefly with the object of securing co-operation against the English, but without success. The State of Travancore, on the southern part of the Malabar Coast, which had never been conquered by Haidar Alī, was invaded by Tīpū at the end of 1789, and as the Rājā of the State was an ally of the British, war once more became inevitable.

In the Third Mysore War, which commenced in 1790, united action was taken against Tīpū by the British, the Marāthās and the Nizām. The British army under Lord Cornwallis took Bangalore in March 1791 and the capital Seringapatam in February 1792. By the treaty, which Tīpū was forced to conclude, Malabar, Coorg, Dindigul and part of the Carnatic, were ceded to England, the Marāthās received the territory between the river Kistna and its southern tributary the Tungabhadra, while the Nizām had certain former possessions restored, including the Cuddapah district; in addition a very heavy indemnity was levied.

During the remaining years of his reign Tīpū did everything in his power to bring about the overthrow of the British power in India, and once more made an unsuccessful attempt to obtain the assistance of the French, sending for this purpose a special embassy to Mauritius. This and other trouble led to the Fourth and last Mysore War, in which, after a short campaign, Seringapatam fell to the assault of the British army under General Harris on 4th May 1799, and Tīpū Sultān was amongst the slain. After Tīpū's death portions of his dominions were divided among the allies, and the Hindu Rāj of Mysore was restored in the person of Krishna Rājā Wodeyar, then a child of six years.

It is difficult to form an accurate estimate of the character of Tīpū Sultān, because the views of contemporary writers, whether English or Muhammadan, are obviously biassed. His cruelty and religious bigotry are undoubted, and he perpetrated many atrocities in the name of religion; he has been justly censured for his excesses in war, though they perhaps never exceeded a standard set elsewhere in more modern times. That he was a brave man cannot be doubted, and while on several occasions he showed considerable military ability, he fell far short of his father in this respect. Unlike Haidar he was a man of education and the changes which he introduced into the calendar, the names of his forts, of civil and military offices, and of weights and measures, certainly display a considerable amount of ingenuity, though by more than one writer they have been held to afford evidence of his insanity. Nowhere else is Tīpū's love of innovation better seen than in his coinage. It has been left to an English writer of fiction to give, in the words of one of his characters, the most favourable account of Tīpū Sultān that I have been able to discover, and while no doubt reproducing contemporary Muhammadan opinion, it is perhaps nearer the truth than are some of the accounts which have been written in an entirely opposite direction. This imperfect notice may fittingly conclude with the extract in question:—

"He was a great man—such an one as Hind will never see again. He had great ambition, wonderful ability, perseverance, and the art of leading men's hearts more than they were aware of, or cared to acknowledge; he had patient application, and nothing was done without his sanction, even to the meanest affairs, and the business of his dominions was vast. You will allow he was brave, and died like a soldier. He was kind and considerate to his servants, and a steady friend to those he loved. Mashalla! he was a great man."—Meadows Taylor, *Tippoo Sultaun*, p. 450.

COINS OF HAIDAR ALĪ.

It was not till after the capture of Nagar or Bednūr, in 1763, that Haidar felt himself sufficiently established in the government of Mysore to undertake the sovereign right of coinage. He did so, however, with extreme caution, for none of his coins exhibits more than the initial letter of his name, and in associating it with Hindu deities he showed remarkable toleration on the part of a Muhammadan; but no doubt he felt it necessary to avoid giving offence to the Hindu population of Mysore which far exceeded his co-religionists in number.

His earliest coin, the so-called Bahādurī pagoda, which judging from its comparative abundance at the present day must have had an extensive circulation, was copied from the pagoda struck in the sixteenth century by Sadāsiva Nāyak, the first Rājā of Ikkeri or Bednūr, who in turn imitated the pagoda of Sadāsivarāya of Vijayanagara (*Cf.* Hultzsch, *Ind. Antiq.*, vol. XX, p. 307, 1891). The rare half-pagoda (No. 6 of the catalogue), referred to briefly by Marsden and so far as I know not chronicled since, in place of Siva and Parvatī has a seated figure of Vishnu, and was no doubt copied from the 'Dūrga' pagoda, coined according to Elliot by the Bedar Poligar of Chitaldrūg, which again followed a Vijayanagara model in the gold coins of Krishnarāya. The "new Muhammad Shāhi" pagoda struck at Gooty (No. 3), was simply a copy of an earlier Mughal pagoda of the same mint which was first coined during the reign of Muhammad Shāh, and was reissued later by Morāri Rāo, the Marāthā chief who occupied Gooty before Haidar. Similar Mughal pagodas were issued at Imtiyaz-garh (Adōni in the Bellary district), Tadpatri (Anantapūr district) and Ganjikōtah (Gandikōta in the Cuddapah district), originally in the reign of Farrukh-Siyar. The second of the Gooty pagodas (No. 4) is dated 1198, and was, therefore, struck in the second year of the reign of Tīpū Sultān, who was in all probability unaware of its existence. I have, for convenience, placed it beside the other Gooty pagoda, although it cannot be regarded as a coin of Haidar Alī.

Two types of gold fanam are met with, the first resembling the Bahādurī pagoda and half-pagoda, the second dated. Among the latter is a coin struck at Calicut dated 1166 (1752-53 A.D.), an impossible date for this town which did not fall into Haidar's hands till 1766; the date is obviously blundered and it is possible that this fanam was really issued by Tīpū Sultān. Tufnell and other writers have referred to coins weighing three grains or even less, which they regard as half-fanams, but I am inclined to think that these, and similar coins of Tīpū, are really small-sized fanams, with the same amount of gold as the ordinary fanams which owe their larger size to a greater amount of alloy.

The copper paisas with elephant obverse, struck at Seringapatam in the last two years of Haidar's reign, are of considerable interest, as they form the model on which the extensive series of copper coins issued by his son was based.

Under the heading "Doubtful copper coins of Haidar Alī" are included three distinct series, all worthy of special mention. The first consists of three roughly executed and undated paisas, two of which were struck at Bellary and the third at Seringapatam; they may possibly have been issued by Tīpū, although their extreme roughness seems to indicate otherwise. Attention may be drawn to the two ways in which the word Bellary is spelt, and it may be stated that no other coins of this mint are known. The coins with Kanarese numerals are evidently a reissue of the similar coins struck by one of the Mysore Rājas before the Muhammadan usurpation, which from their great abundance at the present day had evidently a very extensive circulation. The original coins, which are of two sizes, weighing approximately 46 grains and 23 grains, bear on the obverse Kanarese numerals from 1 to 33 according to Major Jackson, though personally I have not met with a number higher than 32. The significance of these numerals is unknown, but the opinion has been expressed that they may indicate the years of a reign, and but for the awkward exception just referred to I would have felt inclined to attribute them to Chikka Dēva (1672—1704), or to Krishna Raja Wodeyar (1734—1766). The coins, now catalogued for the first time, bear in addition to the Kanarese numerals, which possibly indicate regnal years, the Arabic numeral ۲ repeated, which is perhaps an indication of value. On the chequered reverse Haidar's initial ح is found, a fact which does not enable us to assign the coins definitely either to the father or the son, but inasmuch as Tīpū had a very extensive copper coinage of his own, it seems more likely that these insignificant pieces were issued by his father, to whose general policy of copying earlier types they also conform. We finally come to the "tiger and battle-axe" coins which were first attributed to Mysore by Moor, and were considered by Marsden to be possibly pattern pieces of Tīpū Sultān that never came into general use. I have catalogued them as issues of Haidar, but there is perhaps just as great probability that they originated with Tīpū, to whose half-paisas, and quarter-paisas they on the whole conform both in weight and size*; their border also is identical with that of many of Tīpū's copper coins. I have never met with a specimen in Mysore, and most of those now found come from Malabar, leading to the suspicion that they may have formed a temporary issue for Calicut.

As already indicated the Bahādurī pagoda is still a common coin, while the corresponding half-pagoda is rare, as are also the Gooty pagodas. The half-pagoda with a seated figure of Vishnu is also a rare coin, and I only know of two other specimens than that referred to by Marsden; there was probably a pagoda of similar type, though no examples are known to numismatists. The Bahādurī fanams are not rare, but the other gold fanams are seldom met with. Of the two dated paisas, the one issued in 1195 is not uncommon, while the later one is very rare. The thick coarse paisa struck at Seringapatam is not rare, nor is the Bellary paisa

* The smallest "lion and battle-axe" coin is only about half the weight of Tīpū's eighth of a paisa, and it was possibly intended to represent a sixteenth of a paisa.

with the elephant to right, but the one with the elephant to left is distinctly rare. None of the small copper coins with Kanarese numerals and Haidar's initial is commonly met with, and clear examples showing more than a small part of the die are rare. The "tiger and battle-axe" coins are all rare and particularly those of the smallest size.

HAIDAR ALĪ

Metal. Number.	Date.	Obverse.	Reverse.
		PAGODA.	
AV 1 M	...	Haidar's initial ح on a granulated field. Weight 51·5 grs. Pl. I.	Siva seated with Parvatī on his left knee; in one of the God's right hands a trisul and in one of the left a deer.
2	...	As on No. 1, but the initial letter reversed ح	As on No. 1.
3	1194	محمد شاه .. شـــاه ١١٩٤ ... In a dotted circle. W. 41 grs. Pl. I.	كوتي ضرب On a field ornamented with four-dotted rosettes. The letter ت is not visible in the only example I have seen.
4	1198	As on No. 3, but date ١١٩٨	As on No. 3.
		Although this coin was actually struck during the reign of Tīpū I have preferred to keep it here, as it is a direct continuation of a peculiar issue of Haidar.	
		HALF-PAGODA.	
5	...	As on No. 1. W. 26·5 grs. Pl. I.	As on No. 1.
6 M	..	As on No. 1. W. 26 grs. Pl. I.	Vishnu seated; on his right side a *chakra* (discus) and on the left a *sankha* (conch).
		FANAM.	
7 M	...	As on No. 1. W. 5·5 grs. Pl. I.	As on No. 1.

FANAM—*cont.*

Metal. Number.	Date.	Obverse.	Reverse.
AI 8 M	1189	Haidar's initial ح On a plain field. In a dotted circle. W. 2·7 grs. Pl. I.	١١٨٩ سنه On a plain field. In a dotted circle.
9	1196	As on No. 8.	As on No. 8, but date ١١٩٦
10	...	Haidar's initial ح on a plain field. In a lined circle with a row of dots. W. 5·5 grs. Pl. I.	١١٦٦ كليكو Traces of a lined circle.

The date ١١٦٦ is possibly an error for ١١٩٦ or ١١٩٩; if the latter date was the one intended the coin was struck by Tīpū Sultān.

PAISA.

Metal. Number.	Date.	Obverse.	Reverse.
Æ 11 M	1195	Elephant advancing to right with uplifted tail. W. 191·5 grs. 183·2 grs. Pl. I.	پٹن ب ١١٩٥ ضرب سنه On a field ornamented with dotted rosettes.
12 M	1196	As on No. 11. W. 187 grs.	As on No. 11, but date ١١٩٦

DOUBTFUL COINS OF HAIDAR ALI.

PAISA.

Metal. Number.	Date.	Obverse.	Reverse.
13 M	...	Elephant advancing to right with uplifted tail. W. 187·7 grs. 191·5 grs. 201·5 grs. Pl. I.	بلاري ضرب On a field ornamented with dotted rosettes. In a lined circle.

Metal. Number.	Date.	Obverse.	Reverse.

DOUBTFUL COINS OF HAIDAR ALI—*cont.*

PAISA—*cont.*

Metal. Number.	Date.	Obverse.	Reverse.
Æ 14 M	...	Elephant advancing to left with uplifted tail. W. 201 grs. Pl. I.	باهاري ضرب On a field with dotted rosettes. In a lined circle.
15 M	...	Elephant advancing to right with uplifted tail. Traces of a lined circle. W. 194·5 grs. Pl. I.	پټن ضرب On a field ornamented with dotted rosettes. Traces of a lined circle.

COINS WITH KANARESE NUMERALS.

Number	Date.	Obverse.	Reverse.
16	...	Arabic numerals ٢٢٢ with above them the Kanarese numeral ೯ (9 reversed). In a dotted circle. W. 21·8 grs. 24 grs.	Double cross-lines with the letter ح in one or more of the interspaces.
17	...	Arabic numerals ·٢·٢·٢· with a dot on either side of each: both above and below them the Kanarese numerals ೧೦ (10). In a dotted circle. W. 20·5 grs. 22·0 grs. 22·5 grs. Pl. I.	As on No. 16, with dotted rosettes in the other interspaces.

In some examples the dots at the sides of the Arabic numerals are missing. The Kanarese numerals may be found inverted in either position.

Metal. Number.	Date	Obverse.	Reverse.
		COINS WITH KANARESE NUMERALS—*cont.*	
Æ 18	...	As on No. 17, but Kanarese numerals ററ (11), which in the upper position are inverted. W. 22·0 grs. 23·5 grs.	As on No. 17.
19	...	As on No. 18, but Kanarese numerals ര൭ (12). W. 19·0 grs. 24·5 grs.	Do.
20	...	As on No. 18, but Kanarese numerals ര3 (13).	Do.
21	...	As on No. 18, but Kanarese numerals ര૪ (14). W. 20·0 grs. 20·8 grs.	Do.
		TIGER AND BATTLE-AXE COINS.	
		HALF-PAISA.	
22 M	...	A tiger with uplifted tail standing to right, its face turned towards the spectator. In a double-lined circle with a row of dots. W. 93·5 grs. Pl. I.	A battle-axe with edge to left. In a double-lined circle with a row of dots.
		QUARTER-PAISA.	
23 M	...	As on No. 22. W. 39·0 grs. 43·5 grs. Pl. I.	As on No. 22.
24	...	As on No. 22.	A battle-axe with edge to right. In a double-lined circle with a row of dots.
		EIGHTH-PAISA.	
25	...	As on No. 22. W. 11·2 grs. Pl. I.	As on No. 22.

COINS OF TĪPŪ SULTĀN.

The coins of Tīpū Sultān exist in far greater variety and number than those of his father. They were issued in gold, silver and copper, from no fewer than twelve different mints, and some of them at least appeared in every one of the seventeen years of his reign. But few mint-names occur on Haidar's coins and as far as is known his issues were confined to gold and copper.

THE MINTS.

In the detailed catalogue Tīpū's mints are arranged in the following order:—

(1) Pattan (Seringapatam).
(2) Nagar.
(3) Faiz Hisār (Gooty).
(4) Bengalūr (Bangalore).
(5) Farrukh-yāb Hisār (Chitaldrūg).
(6) Kalīkūt (Calicut).
(7) Farrukhī (Feroke).
(8) Salāmābād (Satyamangalam).
(9) Khāliqābād (Dindigul).
(10) Zafarābād (Gurramkonda).
(11) Khwurshed-sawād (Dhārwār).
(12) Nazarbār (Mysore).

It will be seen from this list that most of the mint-towns, which were selected on account of their military or political importance, bear fanciful names specially invented for them by Tīpū, and that only Nagar, Bangalore, Calicut and Feroke, are recognizable on the coins. One of the mints appears under two designations, viz., its own proper name Dhārwār and the fanciful one Khwurshed-sawād.

Moor (*Narrative of the Operations of Little's Detachment*, p. 476, pl. II, fig. 6) describes and figures a paisa dated 1217, on which the mint-town is read Benazīr, بی نظیر 'the incomparable', a name given by Tīpū to Hole Honnūr in the Shimoga district of Mysore. This coin has not been rediscovered, and as there is some doubt whether the figure was actually taken from a coin I have omitted the mint from the catalogue. The section of Moor's work dealing with coins was prepared in a hurry and contains not a few inaccuracies, hence in the absence of further evidence the above course is probably the best one to adopt.

In the first year of his reign Tīpū issued but few coins and these only from the Seringapatam and Nagar mints. In the fifth regnal year the number of mints was increased to eight, and in the following year when Tīpū may be said to have been at the summit of his power, the only mint not in operation was Calicut which had been destroyed in the previous year and its place taken by Feroke. During the seventh and eighth years a considerable number of mints still issued coins, but in the ninth year there is a sudden falling off, as a result of the military difficulties in which Tīpū found himself before the decisive siege of Bangalore in 1792. By the treaty which followed the capture of that city Tīpū lost the half of his dominions, and from this time onwards Calicut, Feroke, Dindigul, Gurramkonda and Dhārwār ceased to be in his possession. From the tenth year to the end of the reign coins were only issued from the Seringapatam, Nagar and Gooty mints, and from the last of these only in copper. In the seventeenth or last year of the reign which commenced less than a month before the death of Tīpū, so far as is known only two varieties of copper coin were struck, both at the Nagar mint. With but few exceptions and these confined to gold and silver issues, the name of the mint regularly occurs on the coins of Tīpū Sultān.

Following the example of Haidar Alī, Tīpū has not recorded his own name on any of his coins, though the initial letter of his father's name ح is frequently met with on the gold and silver issues. It is equally noteworthy that the name of the ruling Mughal Emperor, Shāh Ālam II, to whom Tīpū at least nominally owed allegiance, is conspicuous by its absence, and it is said that an offering of the coins which he injudiciously or insolently made evoked great resentment from the Emperor on account of this omission.

THE DATES ON THE COINS.

The coins issued during the first four years of Tīpū's reign bear the *Hijri* date, the numerals as usual reading from left to right, while those from the fifth year to the end of the reign are dated in accordance with Tīpū's special *Maulūdi* era, and the figures read from right to left. The coins of the fourth year are dated ١٢٠٠ (1200 A.H.), while those of the fifth year bear the date ٥١٢١ (1215 A.M.), and it appears probable that the commencement of a new century influenced Tīpū in making the change at this time. The *Hijri* years are lunar years of twelve lunar months each, while those of the *Maulūdi* system, which as the name indicates dates from the birth and not from the flight of the Prophet, are luni-solar years of twelve lunar months, with an intercalated or *adhika* month added at certain intervals. Tīpū in founding his new calendar, as was pointed out by Kirkpatrick in 1811, simply adopted the Hindu calendar in common use in Mysore, which had a cycle of sixty years, and substituted Arabic names for the Hindu ones assigned to the cyclic years and months.

The following extract is taken from an article on the subject by the present writer [*Journ., As. Soc., Bengal (New Series)*, Vol. X, 1914]:—"Several writers puzzled by the difference of fourteen years between the two systems at the time the new one was introduced, have supposed that the term Maulūdī was used in a figurative sense, and that the era originated in the commencement of Muhammad's mission, or had reference to the time when he first announced himself as the Messenger of God. The true explanation was, however, furnished by Marsden (*Numismata Orientalia*, Part II, p. 701, 1825) who pointed out, that if the year of the Prophet's birth in the Christian reckoning be subtracted from the Christian year in which the innovation was introduced, the result is 1215. For this purpose Marsden takes the date of Muhammad's birth as 571 A.D., and the first year of the new era as 1786 A.D. (1786 — 571 = 1215); but as we shall see, Tīpū Sultān, for some unexplained reason, appears to have assumed that Muhammad was born in 572 A.D., as the first year of the new era certainly commenced in 1787 A.D. The correct formula is, therefore, 1787 — 572 = 1215.

All writers on the subject since the time of Marsden have, so far as I know, without a single exception, assumed, not unnaturally, that because the fourth regnal year terminated in 1786 A.D., the year 1215 A.M., also commenced in the same year, but this, as I shall proceed to show, is an error and the year 1215 really commenced in 1787. In certain of Tīpū's letters referred to in Kirkpatrick's *Select Letters of Tippoo Sultān* (1811), Beatson's *View of the Origin and Conduct of the War with Tippoo Sultān* (1800), and Wood's *Review of the War in Mysore* (1800), the complete Maulūdī date, and the corresponding Hijrī one, were both noted at the time the letter was written. At my instance these dates have been examined by the Hon'ble Diwan Bahadur L. D. Swamikannu Pillai, M.A., LL.B., author of *Indian Chronology* (Madras, 1911), and a well-known authority on the subject. He reports that they completely establish the facts that the months of Tīpū's new system were Indian lunar months, that the days of the month were simply *tithis* continuously numbered from one to thirty, the fortnights being omitted, and further that Tīpū's extra months were without a single exception the Indian *adhika* months. Mr. Swamikannu Pillai finds that the Maulūdī year began regularly at the same time as the Indian luni-solar year, i.e., on *Chaitra śukla pratipadā*, or the first *tithi* of the bright fortnight of Chaitra, and that the serial numbers of Tīpū's cyclic years, recorded on many of his gold and silver coins, are exactly the same as those of the South Indian cyclic years."

Although an examination of the dates on these letters shows clearly that the *Maulūdi* year 1215 corresponds to 1787–88, yet Marsden, who has been followed by all later writers, makes it commence in 1786, and similarly antedates by one year all the other regnal years of Tīpū Sultān, with but one exception. This exception is the last year of the reign 1227, and concerning the Nagar paisa bearing this date he writes (*op. cit.* p. 724):—"This is probably the latest specimen of his coinage that has been preserved and must have been struck within about a month of his death; the year 1227 of his era having begun on the 6th of April 1799, and the storming of Seringapatam, on which occasion he fell, having happened on the 4th of May of that year, being the anniversary of his accession." So firmly, however, had the mistaken dates become established, that the late Major Tufnell, in his *Catalogue of Mysore Coins in the Collection of the Government Museum, Bangalore* (1889), attempts to show that Marsden is wrong and that the year 1227 corresponds to 1798.

While the fifth regnal year 1215 A.M. commenced on 20th March 1787, the first day of the Indian luni-solar year which was numbered 41 both in the Indian and in Tīpū's calendar, the fourth regnal year 1200 A.H. terminated on 23rd October 1786. On making the change Tīpū was, therefore, forced to allow a period of nearly five months to elapse between the end of the last *Hijri* year and the beginning of the first *Maulūdi* one. If coins were struck during this transitional period they may have been dated 1215 in anticipation of the new era, or it is possible that the coins of 1201 from the Seringapatam, Nagar and Chitaldrūg mints were issued at this time. It is, however, just as likely that the latter coins were dated in error, the die-engraver being unaware of the introduction of the new era. On page 28 will be found a table showing the date according to the Christian reckoning of the commencement of each year of Tīpū Sultān's reign.

As the result no doubt of unfamiliarity with the Arabic numerals on the part of South Indian die-engravers, numerous errors occur in the dates of the coins, more particularly of the copper ones. On the coins of 1215 A.M., the date was intended to be written ٥١٢١ but in a good many cases it is ١٢١٥, as in the older arrangement, and some instances occur of a similar mistake in 1216 and later years. In a few coins the date recorded is a mixture of the two arrangements, e.g., ٢٠٢١ for ٠٢٢١ (*vide* No. 292), while errors due to one or more numerals being reversed are not uncommon, such as ١٢٦٠ for ١٢٢٠, written from left to right in error (No. 118), and ٣١٦٦١ for ٣٢٢١ (No. 332).

The Names of the Cyclic Years.

In arriving at the names of the cyclic years which are found on certain of his gold and silver coins, * Tīpū resorted to two systems in which a certain numerical value is assigned to the letters of the Arabic alphabet. The older of these systems, in use long before Tīpū's time, termed the *abjad*, ابجد a combination of the letters ا ب ج د, contained twenty-two different numbers, nine units, nine tens and the first four hundreds, which were consecutively denoted by the twenty-two Arabic letters that correspond to those of the Hebrew alphabet. As Arabic contains six letters which are not found in the Hebrew alphabet, the last five hundreds and the number one thousand were consecutively assigned to these letters. Tīpū being dissatisfied with the older arrangement, introduced at the same time as his new *Maulūdi* era the system which is known as *abtath*, ابتث from the first four letters of the Arabic alphabet ا ب ت ث, a system in which the same twenty-eight numbers are assigned consecutively to the twenty-eight letters of the Arabic alphabet. These systems of cyclic years were first elucidated by Kirkpatrick and Marsden, but more recently a very clear account, from which the foregoing details are taken, has appeared in the work of Taylor. A reference to any of these writers will show how the numerical value of each cyclic year-name is arrived at. The following table gives the names of the cyclic years for the

---

* The coins on which they occur are the ahmadī, sadīqī, double-rupee, rupee and half-rupee, of the Seringapatam, Nagar, Calicut and Dhārwār mints.

different years of Tīpū's reign, though only those marked with an asterisk are actually known on coins :—

Regnal year.	Cyclic year.	Name of cyclic year.	
1	37	زكي	*zaki*, pure.
2	38	ازل	* *azal*, beginningless eternity.
3	39	جلو	* *jalaū*, splendour.
4	40	دلو	* *dalv*, the sign Aquarius.
5	41	شا	* *shā*, a king.
6	42	سارا	* *sārā*, fragrant.
7	43	سراب	* *sarāb*, a mirage.
8	44	شتا	* *shitā*, winter.
9	45	زبرجد	* *zabarjad*, a topaz.
10	46	سحر	* *sahar*, dawn.
11	47	ساحر	*sāhar*, a magician.
12	48	راسخ	* *rāsikh*, firm.
13	49	شاد	* *shād*, joyful.
14	50	حراست	* *hirāsat*, a guard.
15	51	ساز	*sāz*, concord.
16	52	شاداب	*shādāb*, moist.
17	53	بارش	*bārish*, rain.

NOTE.—The first four regnal years follow the *Abjad* and the remainder the *Abtath* system.

Although the later nomenclature did not come into regular use till the fifth year, *abtath* terms had been invented for the earlier years, and the first regnal year is recorded on the coins as سخ sakh, glass beads, when the date of accession is given.

THE NAMES OF THE MONTHS.

Two systems of nomenclature were adopted by Tīpū for the twelve months of the year. The first, in which the names follow the *abjad* system, was in use during the first four years of the reign ; while the second, which follows the *abtath* system, came into force in the fifth regnal year, along with the *Maulūdi* system of dating the coins. For details as to the two sets of month-names the reader is referred to the works of Kirkpatrick, Marsden and Taylor. On many of Tīpū's ahmadīs, sadīqīs, double-rupees, rupees and half-rupees, struck after the introduction of the *Maulūdi* era, the following words are found on the reverse :—

تاريخ جلوس سال سخ سيوم بهاري

'date of accession : the year Sakh, third of Baharī.'

Baharī is the name of the second month of the year in both systems, and Sakh, سخ glass beads, in the *abtath* reckoning, has the numerical value 37. These coins, therefore, record the fact that Tīpū Sultān ascended the throne on the third day of the second month of the thirty-seventh cyclic year. This year commenced on the 2nd of April 1783, and the date of Tīpū's enthronement therefore corresponds to the 4th May 1783, a period in which, as Marsden points out, 'he was flushed with the victory recently obtained over a British Army, on the Malabar coast.' Curiously enough this day was also the one on which Tīpū died sixteen years later.

In several cases two different regnal years are found on coins bearing the same date. For example two rupees (Nos. 53 and 54) bear the date 1216, while one purports to be of the sixth regnal year and the other of the seventh. The difference is simply due to the fact that the first was struck before the anniversary of Tīpū's accession on 4th May in the year 1216 which commenced on 7th April 1788, while the other appeared between 4th May 1788 and the end of the year 1216 on 26th March 1789. A double-rupee recorded by Weyl (No. 42), bears the date 1198, the cyclic year جلو and the regnal year 3 ; in this case the date is an error for 1199.

The Letter Years.

The copper coins issued from the Seringapatam, Nagar and Gooty mints during the last four years of Tīpū's reign, and no other mints were in operation during these years, bear respectively the first four letters of the Arabic alphabet. The coins of 1224 carry the letter ا, those of 1225 the letter ب, of 1226 the letter ت and of 1227 the letter ث. The letter is placed above the elephant on the obverse, while the date occurs on the reverse and occasionally on the obverse as well. In several coins of the Gooty or Faiz Hisār mint, the letter and date do not correspond, and it seems safest to suppose that the former is correct ; in a strangely blundered quarter-paisa of this mint, bearing the letter ب, different dates are found on the two surfaces and neither of them agrees with the letter.

The Names of the Coins.

Some time after the introduction of the *Maulūdi* era Tīpū Sultān invented names for his coins, on the reverse of which they are usually found, and we owe to Dr. E. Hultzsch (*Ind. Antiq.*, vol. XVIII, p. 313, 1889) the first detailed explanation of these names. The gold and silver coins are called after Muhammadan saints, Khalīfas in the former coins and Imāms in the latter, while the copper coins, with the single exception of the first name for the double-paisa, which is that of a Khalīfa, bear the Arabic or Persian names of stars. The coins and their titles are as follows :—

The four-pagoda piece or *ahmadī*, أحمدي

Ahmad, the 'most praised' is one of the names of the Prophet himself.

The double-pagoda or *sadiqi*, صديقي

Sadiq, 'just,' is derived from Abū Bakr Sadīq, the first Khalīfa.

The pagoda or *fārūqi*, فاروقي

Fārūq, 'timid,' comes from Omar Fārūq, the name of the second Khalīfa.

The double-rupee or *haidari*, حيدري

Haidar, 'a lion,' the designation of Alī, who was both the fourth Khalīfa and the first Imām. Tīpū's father is also commemorated in the name.

The rupee or *imāmi*, امامي

This name which is derived from the word *Imām*, 'leader,' is no doubt intended to stand for the twelve Imāms.

The half-rupee or *ābidi*, عابدي

This name is derived from Alī Zain al Ābidīn, the fourth of the twelve Imāms.

The quarter-rupee or *bāqiri*, باقري

The name of this coin is taken from Muhammad al Bāqir, Muhammad the Great, the fifth Imām.

The one-eighth rupee or *jafari* جعفري

This name is derived from that of Jafar al Sādiq, Jafar the Just, the sixth Imām.

The one-sixteenth rupee or *kāzimi*, كاظمي

This name commemorates Mūsā al Kāzim, Mūsā the Silent, the seventh Imām.

The one-thirty-second rupee or *khizri*, خضري

The name of this, the smallest of the silver coins, is derived from Al Khizr, 'the green one,' a saint who is said to have drunk of the fountain of life and in consequence to be still alive.

The double-paisa, *othmāni* عثماني، or *mushtari*, مشتري

The largest of the copper coins bears two names; the first, which was in use from 1218 up to 1221, commemorates *Othmān* the third Khalīfa, while the second, which first came into use in the year 1221 and was continued in all the later years during which double-paisas were struck, is derived from *al mushtari*, the Arabic name of the planet Jupiter.

The paisa or *zohra*, زهره

This term is simply the Persian name of the planet Venus. The paisas struck at Seringapatam, with one exception (No. 121) and those of Gooty show the above or Persian spelling of the word, while those of the Nagar mint and the exception just referred to bear the designation *zohrā* زهرا the Hindustani spelling.

The half-paisa or *bahrām*, بهرام

This is the Persian name of the planet Mars.

The quarter-paisa or *akhtar*, اختر

This is the Persian word for a star.

The one-eighth paisa or *qutb*, قطب

This is the Arabic name of the Pole Star.

The only one of Tīpū's coins on which no name is ever recorded is the gold fanam, and the omission can hardly be due to the small size of the coin, for the designation khizrī appears on the still smaller silver half-anna. These special coin-names first appear on the gold and silver coins on or after the year 1216, while in the case of the copper coins, with the exception of the double-paisa, which bears the designation othmānī as early as 1218, the names do not appear till 1221, and, as already remarked, the name of the double-paisa was then altered to mushtarī.

THE GOLD COINS.

Of the four varieties of gold coin issued by Tīpū Sultān, the ahmadī was struck at the Seringapatam and Nagar mints, while the sadīqī is only known from the first of these. Judging from the very small number of these coins now procurable their issue cannot have been extensive; on the other hand the pagodas and fanams, which conformed to the general South Indian gold currency, were evidently much more extensively coined. Pagodas were struck at Seringapatam, Nagar and Dhārwār (including Khwurshed-sawād), while fanams, in addition to the three mints just mentioned, omitting Khwurshed-sawād, were also struck at Calicut, Feroke and Dindigul. Both Moor and Hawkes refer to a double gold muhr, which neither of these writers had seen, and the coin has not been recorded by anyone else; according to Hawkes it was known as an 'emaumi.'

AHMADĪ.

This coin, which has an average weight of 211 grains, was probably intended to be the equivalent of four pagodas, as the normal weight of one of the latter coins is 52½ grains. If, however, the weight of 160 grains assigned by Jackson to an ahmadī dated 1198 * (*Coin Collecting in Mysore*, p. 18) is correct, it may be that when the coin was first issued it was intended to correspond

* Hawkes (*Coinage of Mysore*, p. 6) in referring to an ahmadī of the same year, states that 'it weighs about 212 grains of which nearly 182 are pure gold.'

to the muhr or gold rupee, which would weigh approximately 175 grains. In any case the coin is frequently, if incorrectly, termed a gold muhr. Three variations in the inscriptions are met with, and for the first of these the following may be taken as a typical example :—

1. *Obverse.*

احمد
دین در جهان
اســـت
ح ضرب پتن
روشن زفتح حیدر
۱۱۹۸
سال ازل سنه هجر

Reverse.

هو
السلطان
حیـــد
الوالعادل سیوم بهار
۲
سال ازل سنه جلوس

Obv.—The religion of Ahmad is illumined in the world by the victory of Haidar ح. Struck at Pattan, the (cyclic) year Azal (38), the Hijrī year 1198.

Rev.—He is the Sultān, the Unique, the Just. The third of Bahārī, the (cyclic) year Azal (38), the regnal year 2.

The following is the arrangement in the second type :—

2. *Obverse.*

احمد
دین در جهان
اســـت
ح ضرب پتن
روشن زفتح حیدر
شا
۱۲۱۵
سال سنه محمد

Reverse.

As in the first type, but cyclic year شا and regnal year ٥

Obv.—The religion of Ahmad is illumined in the world by the victory of Haidar ح. Struck at Pattan, the (cyclic) year Shā (41), the year 1215, Muhammad.

Rev.—He is the Sultān, the Unique, the Just. The third of Bahārī, the (cyclic) year Shā (41), the regnal year 5.

In this case the name of the cyclic year occupies a line by itself on the obverse, and the word Muhammad is found at the end of the legend on the same surface.

The following is the arrangement in the third and last type :—

3. *Obverse.*

محمد

احمد

دين در جهان

آســــت

ح ضرب

روشن زفتح حيدر احمد

۷۱۲۱

پتن سال سراب سنه

Reverse.

هو الو

السلطان

حيــد

تاريخ سال سخ

العادل جلوس سـ

۷

سيوم بهاري سنه جلوس

Obv.—Muhammad. The religion of Ahmad is illumined in the world by the victory of Haidar ح. An ahmadī struck at Pattan, the (cyclic) year Sarāb (43), the (Maulūdī) year 1217.

Rev.—He is the Sultān, the Unique, the Just. Date of accession the (cyclic) year Sakh (37), the third of Baharī. Regnal year 7.

The name Muhammad now appears at the head of the obverse inscription and the denomination of the coin is also found on the same surface. Marsden remarks, with regard to the inclusion of the name of the Prophet, 'it seems intended to stop the murmurings of those to whom the exclusion of the *hejrah* could not fail to give occasion of scandal, and who might have begun to suspect their sovereign of heterodoxy.' The complete record of Tīpū's accession to the throne is now found on the reverse.

The three types in regard to inscriptions given above are met with in the two larger gold coins, including the one just described, and in the three larger silver coins. While the third type occurs in all of these coins, the first type is only known in the ahmadī, double-rupee and rupee, and the second in the ahmadī, double-rupee and half-rupee; but it is quite probable that this list is incomplete.

SADĪQĪ.

The average weight of this coin is 106 grains and it was probably intended to be equivalent to two pagodas. The reverse inscription and its arrangement are identical with those found on the third type of ahmadī just described, and while the obverse inscription remains the same, the arrangement of the words as shown below is slightly different, making allowance of course for the designation of the coin sadīqī, and the various cyclic years and dates which appear on this surface in the four known varieties of the coin.

Obverse.

محمد

دین احمد در جهان

است

۳

روشن زفتح حیدر صدیقی ضر

٦١٢١

پتن سال سارا سنه

Obv.—Muhammad. The religion of Ahmad is illumined in the world by the victory of Haidar ح. A sadīqī struck at Pattan the (cyclic) year Sāra (42), the (Maulūdī) year 1216.

PAGODA.

Of this coin, generally termed the Sultanī pagoda, which weighs normally 52½ grains, there are three varieties and the last of these bears the distinctive term fārūqī.

1. Struck at the Pattan and Nagar mints in the first four years of the reign, of which the following may be taken as an example:—

Obverse.	*Reverse.*
پتن ٤ ح	هو ن السلطا ١٢٠٠ العادل سنه هجري

On a granulated field.

Obv.—Haidar's initial ح combined with the name of the mint Pattan, and the numeral 4 (regnal year).

Rev.—He is the Sultān, the Just. Hijrī year 1200.

In three coins of this type struck in the years 1197 and 1198 no mint is recorded, and the obverse merely bears Haidar's initial and the numeral denoting the regnal year. As no pagodas issued during these years show the mint-name Pattan, they were in all probability struck at this city. In the Nagar coins the mint-name is placed to the left of Haidar's initial.

2. Struck at the Pattan and Nagar mints in 1215, and at Dhārwār in 1216. The following is an example:—

Obverse.	*Reverse.*
As in var. 1, but regnal year ٥	هو محمد السلطان العا ١٢١٥ دن سنه

Obv.—Haidar's initial combined with the name of the mint Pattan, and the numeral 5 (regnal year).

Rev.—Muhammad. He is the Sultān, the Just. Year 1215.

In the Nagar coin the name of the mint is placed to the left of Haidar's initial, while in the Dhārwār one it is placed below the initial.

3. Struck at Pattan from 1216 to 1223, at Nagar in 1216 and 1217, and at Khwurshed-sawād in 1217 and 1218. As before a Pattan coin is taken as an example.

Obverse.	*Reverse.*
فاروقی	هو محمد
٦	السلطان
پٹح ضرب	حيد
	٦١٢١
	الوالعادل ضرب

Obv.—A fārūqī. Pattan ح (regnal) year 6.
Haidar's initial and the name of the mint are combined.

Rev.—Muhammad. He is the Sultān, the Unique, the Just. Year 1216.

In the Nagar coins the mint-name is to right of Haidar's initial.

The two Khwurshed-sawād fārūqīs show the following inscription on the obverse :—

فاروقح
شيد
خور سواد
٧
ضرب

Obv.—A fārūqī ح Khwurshed-sawād (regnal) year 7.
In this case Haidar's initial is combined with the last letter of fārūqī.

FANAM.

This coin, which weighs from 5 to 6 grains, was equal in value to one-tenth of a pagoda, and in spite of its small size had a considerable circulation in Southern India, where, apart from those issued by Tīpū Sultān, many varieties of fanam exist.

In all Tīpū's fanams the obverse exhibits only Haidar's initial ح within a lined circle and a row of dots, but there are several slight variations in the reverse inscription. In the Pattan fanams we find

١١٩٨ ضرب پتن سنه ١١٩٨ (struck at Pattan in the year 1198), or ١١٩٨ ضرب پتن (struck at Pattan 1198); the first of these arrangements is met with only in the first two regnal years, while the second exists from the second to the thirteenth year. In the Nagar fanams the inscription is similar to the later or second Pattan type, while in those of Calicut it agrees with the first Pattan type, except that the word ضرب is omitted and the last letter of the mint-name occupies a line by itself. The Feroke fanams bear only the mint-name and the date, while the Khāliqābād ones have the date in the middle of the field, with the mint-name above and the word ضرب below. I have never seen a specimen of the Dhārwār fanam and am, therefore, unable to state the arrangement of its inscription.

THE SILVER COINS.

Seven varieties of silver coin were issued by Tīpū Sultān, viz., the double-rupee struck at Pattan, Nagar, and Calicut, the rupee at Pattan, Nagar, Dhārwār and Khwurshed-sawād, the half-rupee at Pattan and Nagar, and finally the quarter, eighth, sixteenth and thirty-second of a rupee, issued only from the Pattan mint.

No silver coins appear to have been struck in the first regnal year, and only coins smaller than the rupee are known after the thirteenth year. The smallest fraction of the rupee or khizrī, was apparently only struck in the twelfth year.

DOUBLE-RUPEE.

This coin which generally weighs from 352 to 355 grains presents three varieties or types as regards its inscriptions, and as these are identical with those already described in detail in the case of the gold ahmadī, it is unnecessary to repeat them. In the double-rupees of the third type, however, the coin-name haidarī appears on the obverse, in place of the word ahmadī found on the gold coin.

The first type of inscription is found on coins dated from 1198 to 1216, including the latter year, while the third type which commences in this same year 1216 is continued to 1220. Of two double-rupees issued from the Nagar mint, one dated 1200 conforms to the earliest type, while the other dated 1215 also belongs to the first type, but shows two variations on the obverse, the word محمد (*Muhammad*) being added to the usual word احمد (*Ahmad*) in the first line, and the word ضرب (struck) being placed before the name of the mint in the last line. The two Calicut double-rupees struck in 1215, which differ chiefly in the arrangement of the figures in the date, are of the second type, but in one of them the name of the cyclic year occurs in the last line on the obverse.

In several of the earlier double-rupees both fields, but more particularly the reverse, are ornamented with conventional floral and even cruciform designs, in addition to the usual rosettes composed of dots; in the later coins the fields are plain.

RUPEE.

This coin weighs on an average 175 grains, but an exceptional specimen may weigh as much as 188 grains. It exists in two types, which except for differences to be detailed presently, agree as regards the inscriptions and their arrangement with the first and third types already noted in the case of the ahmadī and double-rupee. In the coins of the later type the distinctive name imāmī appears on the obverse.

The first type, so far as is known, was issued only from Seringapatam and Nagar, in the year 1200, while the later one appeared from the year 1216 onwards at Seringapatam, and at Dhārwār in 1216. A rupee struck at Nagar in 1216, which must be regarded as a variety of the later type, shows the following variations in the arrangement of the inscriptions; it will be noted that Haidar's initial is omitted :—

Obverse.	*Reverse.*
احمد محمد	هو
دین در جهان روشن	السلطان الوالعادل
است	حید
زفتح حیدر امام ضرب	تاریخ جلوس سال سخ سیوم
٦١٢١	بهار سنه ٦ جلوس
نگر سال سارا سنه	

Obv.—Ahmad. The religion of Muhammad is illumined in the world by the victory of Haidar. An imāmī struck at Nagar, the (cyclic) year Sārā (42), the (Maulūdī) year 1216.

Rev.—He is the Sultān, the Unique, the Just. Date of accession the (cyclic) year Sakh (37), the 3rd of Bahārī. Regnal year 6.

The rupees struck at Khwurshed-sawād in 1217 and 1218 show the following variation in the obverse :—

Obverse.

محمد
احمد
دین درجهان
است
ح ضرب
روشن زفتح حیدر امام
شید سواد سال سراب
خور سنه ٧١٢١

Obv.—Muhammad. The religion of Ahmad is illumined in the world by the victory of Haidar ح. An imāmī struck at Khwurshed-sawād, the (cyclic) year Sarāb (43), the (Maulūdī) year 1217.

HALF-RUPEE.

This coin, the ābidī, weighs about 87 grains and exists in the second and third types already described for several of the foregoing gold and silver coins, but the half-rupee struck at Seringapatam in 1215, is the only known representative of the second type. The Nagar half-rupee agrees with the double-rupee, issued from the same mint in 1215 and already described, in which محمد (*Muhammad*) is added to احمد (*Ahmad*) in the first line of the obverse, and the word ضرب (struck) is found at the commencement of the last line on the same surface.

QUARTER-RUPEE.

Of this coin, otherwise known as the bāqirī, which has an average weight of about 43 grains, and was struck at the Seringapatam mint from 1216 to 1224, only a single type exists with the following inscriptions :—

Obverse.	*Reverse.*
محمد	٦
هوالسلطان	سنه
حيـــــد	باقر
٦١٢١	ب
الوالعادل سنه	ح پتن

Obv.—Muhammad. He is the Sultān, the Unique, the Just. Year 1216 (Maulūdī).

Rev.—Bāqirī (regnal) year 6, ح, Pattan.

EIGHTH-RUPEE.

This coin, the jafarī, with an average weight of about 20 grains, was struck at Seringapatam from 1218 to 1226. The inscriptions are still further reduced.

Obverse.	*Reverse.*
٨١٢١	
سنه محمد	جعفر
	٨
ضرپتح	سنه جلوس

Obv.—Muhammad. Year 1218 (Maulūdī). Struck at Pattan. ح

Rev.—Jafarī. Regnal year 8.

It will be seen that Haidar's initial is combined with the name of the mint.

SIXTEENTH-RUPEE.

This coin, known as the kāzimī, weighs approximately 10 grains, and was issued from the Seringapatam mint in the years 1220 to 1226. Except for the presence of the distinctive name of the coin the inscriptions are identical with those on the eighth-rupee. The following is the arrangement on the reverse :—

کاظمی

۱۰

سنه جلوس

Rev.—Kāzimī. Regnal year 10.

THIRTY-SECOND OF A RUPEE.

This, the smallest of all Tīpū's coins, which weighs approximately 5 grains, was struck at Seringapatam, so far as is known only in the year 1222. It bears the following inscriptions :—

Obverse.	*Reverse.*
السلطنت	۱۲
دار	خضري
ضرب	

Obv.—Struck at the royal residence.*

Rev.—Khizrī (regnal year) 12.

Although no mint-name appears on the coin it may be assumed with some degree of probability, on the analogy of the other small silver coins, that the khizrī emanated from Seringapatam.

THE COPPER COINS.

Copper coins in five different values, viz., double-paisa, paisa, half-paisa, quarter-paisa and eighth-paisa were issued by Tīpū Sultān from no fewer than twelve different mints, though only the paisa appears to have been struck at all of these. The paisa, also, is the only coin known to have been struck in each of the seventeen regnal years.

The copper coins, unlike the gold and silver ones, invariably exhibit on the obverse a figure of an elephant, either advancing or standing with its head to the right or left of the field, † and in some of the double-paisas the animal is represented with its trunk uplifted, as if engaged in the act of *taslīm* or salaaming, an action which it is usually trained to perform on special

---

* I have followed the late Major Tufnell in making the phrase dār al saltanat the equivalent of 'royal residence', rather than of 'capital', as it occurs on coins from four different mints.

† In the Catalogue the terms 'right' or 'left' invariably refer to the right or left of the observer, and not to the heraldic or *proper* right and left.

occasions. It is generally fully caparisoned, with an elaborately decorated body-cloth and head-covering, and with metal anklets on all its feet, in other words with the ornamental trappings worn by the animal on ceremonial or state occasions. As a general rule to which, however, there are many exceptions, the elephant in the earlier coins up to 1221 is turned to the left, while in the later ones from 1221 onwards it is turned to the right; the exceptions are most frequently met with during the first few years of each of these periods. The elephant, which in India is generally associated with royalty, is an inhabitant of the Mysore jungles and appears on the 'Gajapati' pagoda, which probably originated in the ancient Ganga dynasty of Mysore, a coin which was doubtless well known to Haidar and Tīpū.

The paisa weighs approximately 174 grains and the other copper coins in due proportion. The special designations appear first on the double-paisa in 1218 and on the smaller coins in 1221.

A reference is made elsewhere to the fact that some of the smaller copper coins bear the title of a coin of higher value, and it has been suggested that this was the result of a deliberate intention to raise the value of the coin. It is remarked by Buchanan (*Journey to Mysore*, Vol. I, p. 129, 1807):—"The value of the different coins was frequently changed by the late Sultān in a very arbitrary and oppressive manner. When he was about to pay his troops, the nominal value of each coin was raised very high, and kept at that standard for about ten days; during which time the soldiery were allowed to pay off their debts at the high valuation. After this, the standard was reduced to the proper value." It has, however, always seemed to me more probable that the title of these peculiar coins is the result rather of an error on the part of an ignorant workman who was not familiar with the Arabic letters. It seems hardly likely that a purely temporary measure would be recorded on the coin.

By many writers the double-paisa is described as a forty-cash piece, and the other coins in relative proportion down to the eighth of a paisa which is the equivalent of two-and-a-half cash. The term cash or 'kas' was in use in the Tamil districts of Southern India and was introduced in the copper currency of Mysore after the death of Tīpū Sultān, when Krishna Rājā was placed on the throne, probably to make the coins conform to those of the English East India Company. It is, however, doubtful if the term was used by Tīpū, and we know from contemporary writers that the word 'paisa' was then in general use (*vide* Kirkpatrick, Letter CCXXXIV).

The inscriptions on the copper coins are always of limited extent and are practically confined to the reverse.

DOUBLE-PAISA.

This coin, which weighs from 331 to 352 grains, was struck at Seringapatam and Nagar from 1218 to 1226, at Chitaldrūg in 1218 and 1219, and at Feroke in 1218; specimens without any indication of the date are also known from the first two of these mints. There are three main types of this coin:—

(1) Those issued from all four mints between the years 1218 and 1221, the latter year in the case of Pattan only, of which the following may be taken as an example:—

Obverse.	*Reverse.*
Elephant to right with uplifted trunk. Date ١٢١٨ over the tail. Above the elephant a flag.	عثماني پتن ضرب دارالسلطنت Othmānī struck at the royal residence Pattan.

(2) Those issued from Pattan and Nagar in the years 1222 and 1223, of which the following is an example:—

Obverse.	*Reverse.*
As in type (1) but date ١٢٢٢, and the word مولودي (*maulūdi*) above the elephant.	As in type (1) but name of coin مشتري (*mushtari*).

There is a second double-paisa from the Pattan mint, dated 1221, in which the above obverse (2) is combined with a reverse in which the word mushtarī is found, but not the epithet *dār al-saltanat* (royal residence).

(3) Those issued from Pattan and Nagar in the letter years 1224 to 1226, both included:—

Obverse.	*Reverse.*
Elephant to right with depressed trunk. Above the elephant a flag carrying the letter ا but no date.	پتن ضرب دارالسلطنت ١٢٢٤ مشتري سنه مولود Mushtarī struck at the royal residence Pattan, in the Maulūdī year 1224.

PAISA.

This coin, which as already remarked was struck at all the mints, has an average weight of 174 grains, but examples weighing as little as 160 grains and as much as 193 grains are met with. In the earlier paisas, with the exception of the two earliest Nagar ones, the obverse shows merely the elephant and date, but the Pattan and Nagar coins from 1221 to 1223 (both years included) have in addition the word مولودي *maulūdi*, 'relating to the birth' and two paisas struck at Pattan in the years 1221 and 1222 the words محمد مولود *Muhammad maulūd*, 'the birth of Muhammad.'

The distinctive letter for each year is found on coins of the two mints just mentioned, and also on those of Faiz Hisār, from 1224 onwards, and as late as 1227 in the case of Nagar, but the word *maulūdi* has now disappeared from the obverse. As regards the reverse the earlier coins as a rule merely record the mint, with the word ضرب 'struck at', but on Pattan and Nagar paisas of 1221 and subsequent years the special name of the coin زهره *zohra*, or زهرا *zohrā*, appears, while in those of Faiz Hisār it is only met with in the letter years. In the case of all three mints, during the letter years, the word *maulūdi* is associated with the date on the reverse.

A Feroke paisa struck in 1216 has the word سنه *sanah*, 'year' on the obverse, and according to Jackson a Pattan paisa of 1217 has ٧ سنه on the obverse and the date along with the name of the mint on the reverse. A Nagar paisa of 1197 has the word سنه with the date on the reverse. The reverses of some of the earlier paisas of Calicut record the word بندر *bundar*, 'the port', and in others from this mint the regnal year is stated on the same surface. Undated paisas are known from the Pattan, Nagar, Faiz Hisār and Calicut mints.

HALF-PAISA.

This coin, which was issued from all the mints except Calicut, weighs on an average 87 grains, but variations between 82 and 92 grains are met with. The inscriptions and their arrangement in the half-paisa agree on the whole with those of the paisa, the only important difference lying in the fact that the word *maulūdi* is entirely omitted from the former, except in the case of the half-paisas struck at Nagar in the last three years of the reign.

The special name بهرام *bahrām*, occurs first on Pattan coins in 1221 and on Nagar and Faiz Hisār ones in 1222 and 1224 respectively. Undated half-paisas are known from the Pattan, Nagar, Faiz Hisār and Bengalūr mints.

QUARTER-PAISA.

This weighs on an average 42 grains, but examples are met with weighing from 32 to 49 grains; it appears to have been struck at all the mints except Khwurshed-sawād. A quarter-paisa from the Nagar mint dated 1198 has the date and the word سنه recorded on the reverse; the Calicut coins of the same value have no date on either side and merely the name of the mint-town on the reverse.

The distinctive name اختر *akhtar* appears first on Pattan coins in 1221, but on those of Nagar and Faiz Hisār it rarely occurs till the letter years. In other respects the quarter-paisa agrees with the half-paisa.

Attention is drawn elsewhere to the extraordinary errors which occur in some of the quarter-paisas of Nagar, Faiz Hisār and Khāliqābād, errors not only in the date, but extending even to the name of the coin in the first two of these mints. Undated quarter-paisas are known from the Pattan, Faiz Hisār, Bengalūr, Kalīkut and Khāliqābād mints.

EIGHTH-PAISA.

This the smallest of the copper coins, weighing on an average 21 grains, but occasionally as little as 18 grains, was struck only at the Pattan, Nagar, Bengalūr, Farrukh-yāb Hisār and Salāmābād mints. It appeared as early as the year 1216 and as late as 1226.

The special name قطب *qutb*, is only met with on the later Pattan and Nagar coins, appearing in the first of these as early as the year 1222, and as late as the penultimate letter year 1226, while the only known eighth-paisa from the Nagar mint was issued in the year 1226. A variety is known, possibly struck at Pattan, in which the name of the mint is omitted, although the word *qutb* occurs (*vide* Jackson, pl. II, fig. 405), and another is known without any indication of the date.

THE MILLING OF THE COINS.

While the copper coins of Tīpū Sultān are invariably unmilled, many of his gold and silver coins exhibit a highly peculiar and characteristic milling, similar to that met with in some French coins, and which, therefore, perhaps owes its origin to some of Tīpū's French workmen. It consists of one or two irregular grooves running around the edge of the coin, interrupted at regular intervals by transverse depressions or indentations, in such a manner as to give almost a crenated appearance to the margin. In some cases, possibly as the result of wear, the grooves have disappeared and only the crenations remain. The gold ahmadīs and sadīqīs are all milled, as are also the later pagodas issued after 1215, with an occasional lapse; the pagodas of the earlier series are unmilled. The four larger silver coins, from the double-rupee to the quarter-rupee, appear invariably to be milled, and the few doubtful specimens which are met with probably owe their appearance to undue wear rather than to an original absence of milling. A Seringapatam rupee of 1219 in the collection of the Madras Museum, is peculiar in exhibiting a coarse oblique milling, similar to that met with in some of the East India Company Madras rupees and their fractions which were struck early in the nineteenth century.

ALLIED COINS.

Copper coins of quarter-paisa size, with an elephant on the obverse, but which were evidently not struck by Haidar or Tīpū, are occasionally met with. In one of these which is an obvious copy of Tīpū's quarter-paisas, the elephant is surmounted by a crescent and star, while the reverse bears the mint-name Ganjikōtah (Gandikōta in the Cuddapah district), and the date 1215 (1800–01 A.D.). In others, the reverses which are always incomplete and usually illegible, suggest that they were struck by some of the Chiefs in the Bellary, Anantapūr and Cuddapah districts, who struck coins in the name of the Mughal Emperors. One of these bears the date 1161 (1748 A.D.) above the elephant, and if this is not an error as I strongly suspect, it might be regarded as the proto-type from which Haidar Alī took the elephant obverse. Jackson (*Coin Collecting in Mysore*, pl. II, fig. 484) figures a half-paisa in which the reverse bears the illegible name of a mint and the date 1202 (1787–88 A.D.). This coin, which is not uncommon, has an elephant to right, while a second type exists in which the elephant is to the left; both are possibly local issues of Wallajah, Nawāb of the Carnatic.

TABLE *showing the date according to the Christian reckoning of the commencement of each year of Tipū Sultān's reign.*

Regnal year.	Cyclic year.	Letter year.	Maulūdī year.	First day of Maulūdī year (Hindu New Year's Day).	Hijrī year.	First day of Hijrī year.
I.	37	...	...	......	1197	7th December, 1782.
II.	38	...	...	....	1198	26th November, 1783.
III.	39	...	...	.....	1199	14th November, 1784.
IV.	40	...	...	......	1200	4th November, 1785.
...	...	...	...	......	1201	24th October, 1786.
V.	41	...	1215	20th March, 1787.	...	.....
VI.	42	...	1216	7th April, 1788.	...	......
VII.	43	...	1217	27th March, 1789.	...	.....
VIII.	44	...	1218	16th March, 1790.	...	......
IX.	45	...	1219	4th April, 1791.	...	......
X.	46	...	1220	23rd March, 1792.	...	......
XI.	47	...	1221	13th March, 1793.	...	......
XII	48	...	1222	1st April, 1794.	...	......
XIII.	49	...	1223	21st March, 1795.	...	......
XIV.	50	ا	1224	8th April, 1796.	...	......
XV.	51	ب	1225	29th March, 1797.	...	......
XVI.	52	ت	1226	18th March, 1798.	..	......
XVII.	53	ث	1227	6th April, 1799.	...	......

NOTE.—The dates in the column showing the commencement of each Maulūdī year are taken from page XCV of the *Indian Calendar*, by Sewell and Bālakṛishṇa Dīkshit (1896).

The interval between the fourth and fifth regnal years represents the period between the close of the Hijrī year 1200 (on 23rd October, 1786) and the commencement of the Maulūdī year 1215 (on 20th March, 1787). It corresponds to about the first five months of the Hijrī year 1201.

TABLE *showing the years in which Gold and Silver Coins were struck at the different mints of Tipū Sultān.*

Regnal year.	Year.	Ahmadi.	Sadiqi.	Pagoda.	Fanam.	Double-rupee.	Rupee.	Half-rupee.	Quarter-rupee.	Eighth-rupee.	$\frac{1}{16}$ rupee.	$\frac{1}{32}$ rupee.	Mints.
I.	1197	..	...	x.	1, 2.	..	...	...	...	...	...	...	1. Pattan. 2. Nagar.
II.	1198	1	...	2, x.	1, 2, 6.	1	..	...	...	...	...	.	6. Kalikūt. 7. Farrukhī.
III.	1199	1	...	2	1, 2, 6.	1	...	...	..	.	...	...	9. Khāliqābād. 11. Dhārwār.
IV.	1200	...	...	1, 2.	1, 2, 6.	1, 2.	1, 2.	...	...	...	...	...	11a. Khwurshed-sawād.
V.	1215	1	...	1, 2.	1, 2, 6, 9.	1, 2, 6.	...	1, 2	..	...	...	...	x. No mint on coin.
VI.	1216	2	1	1, 2, 11.	1, 2, 7. 11.	1	1, 2, 11.	1	1	...	..	...	
VII.	1217	1	1	1, 2, 11a.	1, 2, 7, 9.	1	1, 11a.	1	1	...	...	..	
VIII.	1218	1	1	1, 11a.	1, 7.	1	1, 11a	1	1	1	...	...	
IX.	1219	1	1	1	1	1	1	1	...	..	...	...	
X.	1220	...	...	1	1, 2.	1	1	1	...	1	1	...	
XI.	1221	...	...	1	1, 2.	...	...	...	1	1	1	...	
XII.	1222	...	...	...	1	...	...	1	1	1	1	1	
XIII.	1223	...	...	1	1	...	1	...	...	1	1		
XIV.	1224	...	...	...	...	...	...	1	1	...	1	...	
XV.	1225	...	...	...	...	...	...	..	..	1	1	...	
XVI.	1226	...	...	...	...	...	...	...	...	1	1	...	
XVII.	1227	...	...	...	...	...	...	...	.	...	...	...	

TABLE *showing the years in which Copper Coins were struck at the different mints of Tipū Sultān.*

Regnal year.	Year.	Double-paisa.	Paisa.	Half-paisa.	Quarter-paisa.	Eighth-paisa.	Mints.
I.	1197	...	1, 2.	...	...	...	1. Pattan. 2. Nagar. 3. Faiz Hisār. 4. Bengalūr. 5. Farrukh-yāb Hisār. 6. Kalīkūt. 7. Farrukhī. 8. Salāmābād. 9. Khāliqābād. 10. Zafarābād. 11. Khwurshed-sawād. 12. Nazarbār.
II.	1198	...	6	...	1, 2.	...	
III.	1199	...	2, 6.	...		...	
IV.	1200	...	1, 2, 4, 6.	1, 2.	1, 2, 4.	...	
V.	1215	...	1, 2, 3, 4, 5, 6, 9.	1, 2, 3, 4, 5, 9, 10.	1, 3, 4.	...	
VI.	1216	...	1, 2, 3, 4, 5, 7, 8, 10, 12.	1, 2, 3, 4, 5, 8, 10, 12.	1, 2, 3, 4, 5, 7, 8, 9, 12.	1, 4.	
VII.	1217	...	1, 2, 3, 4, 5, 7, 8, 9, 11.	1, 2, 3, 4, 5, 7, 8, 9, 11.	1, 2, 3, 4, 5, 7, 9.	1, 5.	
VIII.	1218	1, 2, 5, 7.	1, 2, 3, 4, 5, 7, 8, 10, 11.	1, 3, 4, 5, 7, 8, 9, 10.	1, 4, 5, 7, 9, 10.	1, 4, 8.	
IX.	1219	1, 5.	1, 2, 4, 5.	1, 4, 5.	1, 4, 5.	4	
X.	1220	1	1, 2, 3.	1	1	...	
XI.	1221	1	1, 2, 3.	1, 2, 3.	1	1	
XII.	1222	1, 2.	1, 2, 3.	1, 2, 3.	1, 3.	1	
XIII.	1223	1, 2.	1, 2.	1, 2, 3.	1, 3.	...	
XIV.	1224	1, 2.	1, 2, 3.	1, 2, 3.	1, 2, 3.	1	
XV.	1225	1, 2.	1, 2, 3.	1, 2, 3.	1, 2, 3.	1	
XVI.	1226	1, 2.	1, 2, 3.	1, 2, 3.	1, 2, 3.	1, 2.	
XVII.	1227	...	2	2	...	...	
...	No date.	1, 2.	1, 2, 3, 6.	1, 2, 3, 4.	1, 3, 4, 6, 9.	1	

I. PATTAN پتن

(The Town.)

The word Pattan is a contraction for Srīrangapattana (Seringapatam) 'the town of the Blessed Ranganātha,' in the southern part of Mysore. Here, on an island in the River Cauvery, has existed from the ninth century a Vishnuvaite temple of great sanctity dedicated to Ranganātha, and as has happened so often under similar circumstances in Southern India, a city in course of time grew up around it. Seringapatam is situated at the western end of an island three miles long, by about one in breadth, and its fortifications, which were originally built by successive Rajās of Mysore who made the city their capital, were extended and greatly strengthened by Haidar and Tīpū. The town was seized by Haidar in 1761, at a time when he was becoming firmly established in Mysore; ten years later it was besieged by the Marathās, who after a blockade of fifteen months, were finally induced to come to terms.

The town in its long history stood many sieges, but only the last two of these need be referred to. A British army under Lord Cornwallis appeared before Seringapatam on 6th February 1792, and eighteen days later Tīpū was forced to capitulate, the terms including the handing over of half his dominions and the payment of a heavy indemnity. The date of the first British siege of Seringapatam, which corresponds to about a month before the close of 1219 A.M., is of considerable numismatic interest, for thereafter the mints of Dindigul, Feroke (which succeeded Calicut), Gurramkonda, and Dhārwār, were no longer in Mysore territory; indeed all of these had ceased to issue coins in the previous year. At the same time the number of Tīpū's mints was greatly reduced, and after 1219 only Seringapatam, Nagar and Gooty, remained in operation. The final siege, under the command of General Harris, commenced on the 5th of April 1799, and on the 4th of May the fort was taken by assault and Tīpū Sultān slain.

As the capital of the State Seringapatam was the most important of the mints established by Tīpū Sultān. Coins of all the values in gold, silver and copper, were struck, and some or other of these were issued during all the regnal years, except the last, which commenced less than a month before Tīpū's death. The coins are usually of superior execution, yet die errors are not unknown. Two gold fanams with blundered dates are recorded and also an incorrectly dated rupee of 1220. A paisa, probably of 1216, is dated 216, and another of 1220 is dated 1260; a quarter-paisa is recorded by Jackson with bahrām (half-paisa) in error for akhtar, and a quarter-paisa of 1225 is wrongly dated 1224. There is a one-eighth paisa dated 1222, with no indication of the mint-town, which in all probability emanated from Seringapatam.

In the catalogue reference will be found to certain special marks, which occur in addition to the usual dotted rosettes on some of the double-paisas, paisas and half-paisas, more particularly of 1224, 1225 and 1226. One of these, which may be described as an obliquely twisted pointed oval, occurs also on Gooty copper coins of 1225 and 1226. What the significance of this mark may have been it is impossible to say, but the fact that it occurs on coins of the same years issued from two different mints, appears to indicate that some importance was attached to it.

The coins in all three metals show a border, which was copied in several of the other mints, consisting of a double-lined * circle enclosing a row of dots, the only exceptions being the double-rupee and rupee of 1219, which exhibit short concentric rays arranged in the form of a circular band.

On the copper coins from the year 1221† onwards, the denomination of value is recorded, that of the paisa being زهرا zohrā in a single case (No. 121), and in all others زهره zohra. In the same year reference is made for the first time to the new era instituted by Tīpū, paisas of 1221 and 1222 bearing the date and the words مولود محمد 'the birth of Muhammad', to be followed in coins of the same years and of 1223 in addition, by the date and the adjectival word مولودي 'relating to the birth.'

As regards the gold coins, specimens of the ahmadī and sadīqī are of great rarity, particularly the latter, but most of the pagodas and fanams are not uncommon. Counterfeit fanams, evidently made when the coins were in circulation, are not uncommon in brass, copper, and even in silver. With the exception of some of the rupees and half-rupees, the silver coins are all scarce, particularly certain of the double-rūpees and the smaller silver issues, notably the khizrī ‡, which is extremely rare.

Many of the copper coins are still found in great numbers, but all the double-paisas, except perhaps that of 1225, and the one-eighth paisas, are rare. The commonest paisas are those issued after 1220, and particularly those of the years 1224 and 1225; of the four varieties struck in 1221, the rarest is No. 121, of those struck in the following year No. 124, and of those of 1223 the rarest is No. 128. The paisas dated 1201 and 216 (for 1216) are both rare. The commonest half-paisas are those of 1224 and 1225, but many of the others are relatively common; among the rarer ones may be enumerated Nos. 140, 148, 151 and 153. Of the two half-paisas of 1216 the larger and thinner coin is the rarer. It may be noted that the half-paisa of 1226, a common coin, is always of coarser fabric than the corresponding coins of the two preceding years. Many of the quarter-paisas are still very common, particularly as in the case of the other copper coins, those of the later years.

---

* In the smaller silver coins there is a single-lined circle forming the inner boundary of a row of dots.

† Jackson records a quarter-paisa of 1219, with the designation bahrām in error for akhtar. I do not know of any other instance of the special name appearing on a quarter-paisa prior to the year 1221, and the record is possibly due to some mistake.

‡ On this coin no mint is recorded, but merely the fact that it was struck at the 'royal residence.' There can, I think, be no doubt that it is an issue of Seringapatam.

PATTAN.

Metal. Number.	Date.	Obverse.	Reverse.
		AHMADĪ.	
AV 1	1198	احمد دین درجهان است ح ضرب پتن روشن زفتح حیدر ۱۱۹۸ سال ازل سنه هجر On a field ornamented with dotted rosettes. In a double-lined circle with a row of dots.	هو السلطان حید ر الو العادل سیرم بهار ۲ سال ازل سنه جلوس On a field ornamented with dotted rosettes. In a double-lined circle with a row of dots.
		(Hawkes.)	
2	1199	As on No. 1, but cyclic year جلو and date ۱۱۹۹	As on No. 1, but cyclic year جلو and regnal year ۳
		(Jackson.)	
3 M	1215	احمد دین درجهان است ح ضرب پتن روشن زفتح حیدر ۱۰۱۵ سال سنه محمد On a field ornamented with dotted rosettes. In a double-lined circle with a row of dots. Pl. I.	As on No. 1, but cyclic year شا and regnal year ۵

PATTAN.

Metal. Number.	Date.	Obverse.	Reverse.
		AHMADĪ—*cont.*	
Al 4	1217	محمد احمد دین درجهان است ضرب ح وشی زفتح حیدر احمد ب ۷۱۲۱ پتن مال سراب سنه In a double-lined circle with a row of dots.	هو الو السلطان حید تاریخ مال سح العادل جلوس س ب ۷ سیوم بهاري سنه جلو In a double-lined circle with a row of dots.
5	1218	As on No. 4, but cyclic year شتا and date ۸۱۲۱	As on No. 4, but regnal year ۸
6 M	1219	As on No. 4, but cyclic year زبرجد and date ۹۱۲۱	As on No. 4, but regnal year ۹
		SADĪQI.	
7	1216	محمد دین احمد درجهان است ح روشن زفتح حیدر صدیقی ضر ب ۶۱۲۱ پتن مال سارا سنه In a double-lined circle with a row of dots.	هو الو السلطان حید تاریخ مال سح العادل جلوس م ب ۶ سیوم بهاري سنه جلو In a double-lined circle with a row of dots.
8 M	1217	As on No. 7, but cyclic year سراب and date ۷۱۲۱	As on No. 7, but regnal year ۷ Pl. I.
9	1218	As on No. 7, but cyclic year شتا and date ۸۱۲۱	As on No. 7, but regnal year ۸
10	1219	As on No. 7, but cyclic year زبرجد and date ۹۱۲۱	As on No. 7, but regnal year ۹

PATTAN.

Metal. Number.	Date.	Obverse.	Reverse.
		PAGODA.	
AV 11	1197	اح On a granulated field. In a double-lined circle with a row of dots.	هو ن السلطا ١١٩٧ هجر العادل سنه In a double-lined circle with a row of dots.
12 AV	1198	As on No. 11, but regnal year ٣	As on No. 11, but date ١١٩٨
13 AV	"	As on No. 11, regnal year ١ (in error for ٣).	As on No. 12. Pl. I.
14 AV	1200	 A combination of Haidar's initial ح with the name of the mint پتن On a granulated field. In a double-lined circle with a row of dots.	As on No. 11, but date ١٢٠٠ Pl. I.

(*Hawkes, pl. II, fig. 3.*)

Metal. Number.	Date.	Obverse.	Reverse.
15 AV	1215	As on No. 14, but regnal year ٥	هو محمد السلطان العــــا ١٢١٥ دل سنه On a field ornamented with dotted rosettes. In a double-lined circle with a row of dots.

PATTAN.

Metal. Number.	Date.	Obverse.	Reverse.
		PAGODA—*cont.*	
Al 16	1216	ناروتـ ب ٦ پتـج سنه Haidar's initial and the name of the mint are combined as before. In a double-lined circle with a row of dots.	هو محمد السلطان حيـــد الو العادل ١ ٦١٢١ سنه In a double-lined circle with a row of dots.
17 M	1217	As on No. 16, but regnal year ٧ Pl. I.	As on No. 16, but date ٧١٢١
18 M	1218	As on No. 16, but regnal year ٨	As on No. 16, but date ٨١٢١
19 M	1219	As on No. 16, but regnal year ٩	As on No. 16, but date ٩١٢١
20 M	1220	As on No. 16, but regnal year ٠١	As on No. 16, but date ٠٢٢١
21 M	1221	As on No. 16, but regnal year ١١	As on No. 16, but date ١-٢١
22	1223	As on No. 16, but regnal year ٣١	As on No. 16, but date ٣٢٢١
		FANAM.	
23 M	1197	ح On a plain field: in a lined circle with a row of dots.	١١٩٧ سنه ضرب پتن ب Dotted rosettes in the lower part of the field: in a lined circle with a row of dots.
24 M	1198	As on No. 23.	As on No. 23, but date ١١٩٨ and on a plain field.

PATTAN

Metal. Number.	Date.	Obverse.	Reverse.
		FANAM—*cont.*	
AR 25	1198	As on No. 23. Pl. I.	١١٩٨ ب ضرب پتن On a plain field. In a lined circle with a row of dots.
26 M	1199	Do.	As on No. 25, but date ١١٩٩
27 M	1200	Do.	As on No. 25, but date ١٢٠٠
28	1201	Do.	As on No. 25, but date ١٢٠١
		(Jackson.)	
29 M	1215	As on No. 23.	As on No. 25, but date ١٢١٥
30	"	Do.	As on No. 25, but date ٥١٢١
31 M	1216	Do.	As on No. 25, but date ٦٠٢١
32 M	1217	Do.	As on No. 25, but date ٧١٢١
33 M	1218	Do.	As on No. 25, but date ٨١٢١
34 M	1219	Do.	As on No. 25, but date ٩١٢١
35	1220	Do.	As on No. 25, but date ٠٢٢١
36	1221	Do.	As on No. 25, but date ١٢٢١
37	1222	Do.	As on No. 25, but date ٢٢٢١
38 M	1223	Do.	As on No. 25, but date ٣٢٢١
39	—	As on No. 23, but Haidar's initial reversed.	As on No. 25, but date ٧١٧١ (possibly in error for ٧١٢١)
		(Jackson.)	

PATTAN.

Metal. Number.	Date.	Obverse.	Reverse.
		FANAM—*cont.*	
AV 40	--	As on No. 23.	As on No. 25, but date represented only by the figures ١٢
		(Tufnell.)	
		DOUBLE-RUPEE.	
AR 41 M	1198	احمد دين درجهان است ضرب پتن ٣ روشن زفتح حيدر ١١٩٨ سال ازل مذ دهر	هو السلطان حيد الو العادل سيوم بهار ٣ سال ازل مذ جلوس
		On a field ornamented with dotted rosettes. In a double-lined circle with a row of dots. Pl. I.	On a field ornamented with dotted rosettes. In a double-lined circle with a row of dots.
		In some examples the field, more particularly on the reverse, is elaborately decorated with floral designs.	
42	"	As on No. 41.	As on No. 41, but cyclic year جلو and regnal year ٣
		(Weyl.)	
43	1199	As on No. 41, but cyclic year جلو and date ١١٩٩	As on No. 42.
44	1200	As on No. 41, but cyclic year دلو and date ١٢٠٠	As on No. 41, but cyclic year دلو and regnal year ٤

PATTAN.

Metal. Number.	Date.	Obverse.	Reverse.
		DOUBLE-RUPEE—*cont.*	
AR 45	1215	As on No. 41, but cyclic year شا and date ١٢١٥	As on No. 41, but cyclic year شا and regnal year ٥
46	1216	As on No. 41, but cyclic year سارا and date ١٢١٦ Pl. I.	As on No. 41, but cyclic year سارا and regnal year ٦
47 M	"	محمد احمد دين درجهان امست ضرب ح روشن زفتم حيدر حيدر ١٢١٦ پتن سال سارا سنه On a plain field. In a double-lined circle with a row of dots. Pl. II.	هو الو السلطان حيد تاريخ سال محع العادل جلوس س ٦ ميوم بهاري سنه جلو On a plain field. In a double-lined circle with a row of dots.
48 M	1217	As on No. 47, but cyclic year سراب and date ١٢١٧	As on No. 47, but regnal year ٧
49	1218	As on No. 47, but cyclic year شتا and date ١٢١٨	As on No. 47, but regnal year ٨
50	1219	As on No. 47, but cyclic year زبرجد and date ١٢١٩ In a rayed circle.	As on No. 47, but regnal year ٩ In a rayed circle.
		(Tufnell, pl. II, 116.)	
51	1220	As on No. 47, but cyclic year سحر and date ١٢٢٠	As on No. 47, but regnal year ١٠

(Marsden.)

PATTAN.

Metal. Number.	Date.	Obverse.	Reverse.
		RUPEE.	
AR 52	1200*	احمد دين درجهان است ح ضرب پتن روشن زفتح حيدر ١٢٠٠ سال دلو سنہ هجر On a field ornamented with dotted rosettes. In a double-lined circle with a row of dots.	هو السلطان حيد الو العادل سيوم بهار ٤ سال دلو سنہ جلوس On a field ornamented with dotted rosettes. In a double-lined circle with a row of dots.
53 M	1216	محمد احمد دين درجهان است ح ضرب روشن زفتح حيدر امام ١٢١٦ پتن سال سارا سنہ On a plain field. In a double-lined circle with a row of dots. Pl. II.	هو الو السلطان حيد تاريخ سال صح العادل جلوس س ٦ سيوم بهاري سنہ جلو On a plain field. In a double-lined circle with a row of dots.

In some examples the field on both sides is ornamented with dotted rosettes. Jackson refers to a variety in which the coin is thicker than usual, with a plain rim instead of the double circle and dots.

54	"	As on No. 53.	As on No. 53, but regnal year ٧

(Weyl.)

* Rice *(Mysore Gazetteer)* refers to a rupee of 1198, but I am inclined to think this is an error as I do not know of any other reference to the coin.

PATTAN.

Metal. Number.	Date.	Obverse.	Reverse.
		RUPEE—*cont.*	
AR 55 M	1217	As on No. 53, but cyclic year سراب and date ٧١٢١	As on No. 53, but regnal year ٧
56 M	1218	As on No. 53, but cyclic year شتا and date ٨١٢١	As on No. 53, but regnal year ٨
57 M	1219	As on No. 53, but cyclic year زبرجد and date ٩١٢١ In a rayed circle. Pl. II.	As on No. 53, but regnal year ٩ In a rayed circle.
		The only specimen of this coin I have seen has an oblique milling.	
58	1220	As on No. 53, but cyclic year سحر and date ٠١٢٢ (in error for ١٢٢٠) *(Weyl.)*	As on No. 53, but regnal year ٩
59	,,	As on No. 58.	As on No. 53, but regnal year ١٠ *(Weyl.)*
60 M	1223	As on No. 53, but cyclic year شاد and date ٣٢٢١	As on No. 53, but regnal year ١٣
		HALF-RUPEE.	
61	1215	احمد دین درجهان اسـ ح بقی روشن ز فتح حیدر ضرب ٥١٢١ سال سنه محمد On a field ornamented with dotted rosettes. In a double-lined circle with a row of dots. *(Taylor, pl. I, fig. 20.)*	هو السلطان حیـد ر العادل میمون بهار ٥ سال شا سنه جلوس On a field ornamented with dotted rosettes. In a double-lined circle with a row of dots.

PATTAN.

Metal. Number.	Date.	Obverse.	Reverse.
		HALF-RUPEE—*cont.*	
AR *62 M	1216	محمد دین احمد درجہان اسـ ـت ضرب روشن زفتح حیدر عابد ١٢١٦ پتن مال سارا سنہ In a double-lined circle with a row of dots.	هو الو السلطان حیـ ـد تاریخ مال مخ العادل جلوس س ٦ سیوم بهاري سنہ جلو In a double-lined circle with a row of dots.
63	1217	As on No. 62, but cyclic year سراب and date ١٢١٧	As on No. 62, but regnal year ٧
64	1218	As on No. 62, but cyclic year شتا and date ١٢١٨	As on No. 62, but regnal year ٨
65	1219	As on No. 62, but cyclic year زبرجد and date ١٢١٩	As on No. 62, but regnal year ٩
66	1220	As on No. 62, but cyclic year سحر and date ١٢٢٠	As on No. 62, but regnal year ١٠
		(Marsden.)	
67 M	1222	As on No. 62, but cyclic year راسخ and date ١٢٢٢	As on No. 62, but regnal year ١٢ Pl. II.
68	1224	As on No. 62, but cyclic year حراست and date ١٢٢٤	As on No. 62, but regnal year ١٤
		(Weyl.)	

* Taylor (*Coins of Tipū Sultān*, p. 27) describes an ābidī of 1215 belonging to the third type on which the name of the coin is recorded, but it bears the cyclic year شتا (1218) and is, therefore, probably the coin numbered 64 in the present catalogue. The coin dated 1215, which he figures on pl. I, fig. 20, belongs to the second type and is No. 61 above.

PATTAN.

Metal. Number.	Date.	Obverse.	Reverse.
		QUARTER-RUPEE.	
AR 69	1216	محمد هو السلطان حيـــــد ١٢١٦ الو العادل سنه In a double-lined circle with a row of dots.	٦ سنه باقر ب ح پتن In a double-lined circle with a row of dots.
70 M	1217	As on No. 69, but date ١٢١٧ Pl. II.	As on No. 69, but regnal year ٧
71 M	1218	As on No. 69, but date ١٢١٨	As on No. 69, but regnal year ٨
72 M	1221	As on No. 69, but date ١٢٢١	As on No. 69, but regnal year ١١
73 M	1222	As on No. 69, but date ١٢٢٢	As on No. 69, but regnal year ١٢
74	1224	As on No. 69, but date ١٢٢٤	As on No. 69, but regnal year ١٤

Jackson records this coin with the regnal year 16, possibly an error on his part.

Metal. Number.	Date.	Obverse.	Reverse.
		EIGHTH-RUPEE.	
75	1218	١٢١٨ سنه محمد ضر پتح In a lined circle with a row of dots. Haidar's initial letter is combined with the name of the mint.	جعفر ب ٨ سنه جلوس In a lined circle with a row of dots.

I have not seen this coin, which is recorded only by Jackson, and have assumed that it is similar to the others of the same series.

Metal. Number.	Date.	Obverse.	Reverse.
		EIGHTH-RUPEE—*cont.*	
AR 76	1220	As on No. 75, but date ١٢٢٠	As on No. 75, but regnal year ١٠
77 M	1221	As on No. 75, but date ١٢٢١ Pl. II.	As on No. 75, but regnal year ١١
78	1222	As on No. 75, but date ١٢٢٢	As on No. 75, but regnal year ١٢
79	1223	As on No. 75, but date ١٢٢٣	As on No. 75, but regnal year ١٣
		(Marsden.)	
80	1225	As on No. 75, but date ١٢٢٥	As on No. 75, but regnal year ١٥
81	1226	As on No. 75, but date ١٢٢٦	As on No. 75, but regnal year ١٦
		(Weyl.)	
		SIXTEENTH-RUPEE	
82	1220	١٢٢٠ سنہ محمد ضرب پتن In a lined circle with a row of dots.	کاظم ١٠ سنہ جلوس In a lined circle with a row of dots.
83 M	1221	As on No. 82, but date ١٢٢١ Pl. II.	As on No. 82, but regnal year ١١
		In some examples Haider's initial is combined with the name of the mint.	
84	1222	As on No. 82, but date ١٢٢٢	As on No. 82, but regnal year ١٢
85	,,	As on No. 84.	As on No. 82, but regnal year ١٦ (in error for ١٢)

(Jackson, pl. II, 395.)

PATTAN.

Metal.	Number.	Date.	Obverse.	Reverse.
			SIXTEENTH-RUPEE—*cont.*	
AR	86	1223	As on No. 82, but date ٣٢٢١	As on No. 82, but regnal year ٤١
			(Marsden.)	
	87	1224	As on No. 82, but date ٤٢٢١	As on No. 86.
	88	1225	As on No. 82, but date ٥٢٢١	As on No. 82, but regnal year ٥١
			In the only example of this coin that I have seen the regnal year is placed in the upper line of the reverse.	
	89	1226	As on No. 82, but date ٦٢٢١	As on No. 82, but regnal year ٦١
			(Weyl.)	
	90	,,	As on No. 82, but date ١٦٦٢ (in error for ٦٢٢١)	As on No. 89.
			(Weyl.)	
			ONE-THIRTY-SECOND RUPEE.	
	91	1222	السلطنت دار ضرب In a lined circle with a row of dots.	٢١ خضري In a lined circle with a row of dots.
			DOUBLE-PAISA.	
Æ	92 M	1218	Elephant advancing to right with uplifted trunk, date ٨١٢١ over the tail which is depressed: above the elephant a flag, with a star in a central square surrounded by a border of dashes. In a double-lined circle with a row of dots. **Pl. II.**	عثماني پتن ضرب دارالسلطنت In a double-lined circle with a row of dots.

PATTAN.

Metal. Number.	Date.	Obverse.	Reverse.
		DOUBLE-PAISA—*cont.*	
Æ 93	1218	As on No. 92, but elephant to left. Pl. II.	As on No. 92, but field ornamented with dotted rosettes.
94	1219	As on No. 92, but date ٩١٢١	As on No. 92.
95 M	,,	As on No. 93, but date ٩١٢١	Do.
		A specimen of this coin in the collection of the Indian Museum, Calcutta, has a five-branched tree-like mark near the lower margin of the reverse and the field of this surface ornamented with dotted rosettes.	
96	1220	As on No. 93, but date ٠٢٢١	As on No. 93.
97	1221	As on No. 93, but date ١٢٢١	As on No. 92.
		(Jackson, pl. II, 380.)	
98 M	,,	Elephant advancing to right with uplifted trunk, date ١٢٢١ over the tail which is depressed: above the elephant a flag, with a central star and four dashes in the corners: between the elephant's back and the flag the word مولودب divided by the flag-staff. Pl. II In a double-lined circle with a row of dots.	مشتری پتن ضرب On a field with dotted rosettes: a special mark below the letter ش In a double-lined circle with a row of dots.

PATTAN.

Metal. Number.	Date.	Obverse.	Reverse.
		DOUBLE-PAISA—*cont.*	
Æ 99 M	1222	As on No. 98, but date ٢٢٢١ and word مولودي to left of the flag-staff. Pl. II.	مشتري پتن ضرب دارالسلطنت On a field with dotted rosettes. In a double-lined circle with a row of dots.

A variety exists with the star on the flag enclosed in a rectangle, and the word مولودي above the elephant, and another is mentioned by Jackson in which the first two letters of مولودي are to right of the flag-staff. Tufnell describes the coin as having the word عثماني on the reverse, but this is probably an error.

Metal. Number.	Date.	Obverse.	Reverse.
100	1223	As on No. 99, but date ٣٢٢١	مشتري پتن ضرب دارالسلطنت On a field with dotted rosettes. In a double-lined circle with a row of dots.
101 M	1224	Elephant advancing to right with depressed trunk and tail: above the elephant a flag, with the letter ا in the centre and four oblique dashes in the corners. In a double-lined circle with a row of dots. Pl. III.	پتن دارالسلطنت ضرب ٤٢٢١ مشتري سنه مولود On a field with dotted rosettes. In a double-lined circle with a row of dots.

There is a variety with two or more oblique pointed oval marks on the reverse which is otherwise plain, and another with a four-rayed star in the lower part of the field.

Metal. Number.	Date.	Obverse.	Reverse.
		Double-Paisa—*cont.*	
Æ 102 M	1225	As on No. 101, but the letter ب on the flag.	As on No. 101, but date ٥٢٢١

There are numerous variations in this coin as regards the reverse which may be plain or ornamented, and in the arrangement of its inscription. The word شتري may be placed entirely below سنه and Jackson records two abnormalities in the position of the date, viz., ٥٢٢١ and .. ا مو ٢ لو ٢ د ٥ .ذ. مولود The pointed oval mark mentioned in connexion with the coin of 1224 may be found, usually in conjunction with a single dotted rosette, either near the upper or near the lower margin; a single dotted rosette is also sometimes found towards the middle of the right-hand margin. A specimen in the collection of the Indian Museum, Calcutta, has a dotted cross near the left margin and in line with the date.

Metal. Number.	Date.	Obverse.	Reverse.
103	1226	As on No. 101, but the letter ت on the flag. *(Jackson.)*	As on No. 101, but date ٦٢٢١
		Paisa.	
104	1197	Elephant to left with uplifted tail: above the elephant a dotted rosette. In a lined circle with a row of dots. *(Neumann.)*	١١٩٧ پتن ضرب On a plain field. In a lined circle with a row of dots.
105 M	1200	Elephant advancing to right with uplifted tail: above the tail the date ١٢٠٠ In a double-lined circle with a row of dots.	پتن ب ضر On a field with dotted rosettes. In a double-lined circle with a row of dots.

PATTAN.

Metal. Number.	Date.	Obverse.	Reverse.
Æ		PAISA—*cont.*	
106 M	1200	Elephant advancing to left with uplifted tail: above the tail the date ١٢٠٠ In a double-lined circle with a row of dots.	As on No. 105.
107 M	1201	As on No. 106, but date ١٢٠١ Pl III.	Do.
108 M	1215	As on No. 106, but date ١٢١٥	Do.
109 M	"	As on No. 106, but date ٥١٢١	Do.
		A variety exists with the last figure of the date above the head of the elephant.	
110	1216	As on No. 106, but date ١٢١٦	As on No. 105.
		(Weyl.)	
111 M	"	As on No. 106, but date ٦١٢١	Do.
		In some copies the reverse field is plain. There are two marked variations in size; in the larger and thinner coin the diameter of the inner circle is 20 mm., in the smaller and thicker coin it is 17·5 mm. In the latter variety the last figure of the date is above the head of the elephant.	
112 M	"	As on No. 105, but date ٦١٢ (probably in error for ٦١٢١)	As on No. 105. On a plain field.
113 M	1217	As on No. 106, but date ٧١٢١	As on No. 105.
114	"	As on No. 106, but above the elephant ٧ سنه	ضرب پتن سنه ٧١٢١
		I have not seen this coin, which is recorded by Jackson, and am unable to state how the inscription on the reverse is arranged.	

PATTAN.

Metal. Number.	Date.	Obverse.	Reverse.
		Paisa—*cont.*	
Æ 115 M	1218	As on No. 106, but date ٨١٢١	As on No. 105.
116 M	1219	As on No. 106, but date ٩١٢١	پٹن ضرب On a field with dotted rosettes. In a double-lined circle with a row of dots.
		A variety exists with a plain reverse.	
117 M	1220	As on No. 106, but date ٠٢٢١	As on No. 116.
118 M	,,	As on No. 105, but date ١٢٠٠ (probably in error for ١٢٢٠) above the elephant's back. Pl. III.	As on No. 112.
119 M	1221	As on No. 106, but date ١٢٢١ Pl. III.	As on No. 116.
		The reverse field is sometimes plain.	
120 M	,,	As on No. 105, but date ١٢٢١ above the elephant's back. Pl. III.	As on No. 112.
121 M	,,	Elephant advancing to left with depressed tail: above the elephant مولود محمد ١٢٢١ In a double-lined circle with a row of dots. Pl. III.	زهرا ب ضر پٹن A dotted rosette in the right upper part of the field. In a double-lined circle with a row of dots.
		There is a variety on a plain field with the ضر of ضرب at the same level as the ب	

PATTAN.

PAISA—*cont.*

Metal. Number.	Date.	Obverse.	Reverse.
Æ 122 M	1221	Elephant advancing to right with uplifted tail: above the elephant ١٢٢١ مولود Pl. III.	زهره پتن ضرب On a field with dotted rosettes. In a double-lined circle with a row of dots.
123 M	1222	As on No. 105, but date ٢٢٢ above the elephant's back.	As on No. 112.
124 M	..	As on No. 121, but date ١٢٢٢	زهره ضرب پتن On a plain field. In a double-lined circle with a row of dots.
125 M	..	As on No. 122, but date ١٢٢٢	زهره ضرب پتن On a field with dotted rosettes. In a double-lined circle with a row of dots.
		There is a variety with the last letter of ضرب nea the lower margin of the reverse, and another in which the first two figures of the date are placed to right of the word مولود	
126 M	..	Elephant advancing to left with depressed tail: above the elephant ٢٢٢ امولود In a double-lined circle with a row of dots.	As on No. 124.

PATTAN.

Metal. Number.	Date.	Obverse.	Reverse.
		PAISA—*cont.*	
Æ 127 M	1222	As on No. 126, but above the elephant ۲۲۲ ،ولودي	As on No. 124.
128 M	1223	As on No. 105, but date ۱۲۲۳ and the first two figures to right of the tail.	As on No. 116, but a plain field.
129 M	,,	Elephant advancing to right with uplifted tail: above the elephant ۲ ۲ ۳ / ا و لو دي In a double-lined circle with a row of dots.	As on No. 128.
130 M	,,	As on No. 122, but date ۱۲۲۳	As on No. 125.
		The following varieties are met with :—(*a*) مولودي (*b*) first two figures of the date to right of مو	
131 M	,,	Elephant advancing to left with depressed tail: above the elephant ۱۲۲۳ مولود In a double-lined circle with a row of dots.	As on No. 124, but field with dotted rosettes.
132 M	,,	As on No. 131, but elephant with uplifted tail, and above the elephant ۱۲۲ مولود ۳	As on No. 131.
133 M	1224	Elephant advancing to right with depressed tail: above it the letter ا In a double-lined circle with a row of dots.	۱۲۲۴ / پٹن مولود / زهره ضرب In a double-lined circle with a row of dots.
		In addition to numerous variations in the arrangement of the figures of the date, the following special marks are also found on the reverse, usually near the lower margin:—(*a*) rosette of seven dots, (*b*) rosette of four dots, (*c*) four-pointed star, (*d*) oblique pointed oval. Pl. III.	

PATTAN.

Metal. Number.	Date.	Obverse.	Reverse.
		PAISA—*cont.*	
Æ 134 M	1225	As on No. 133, but letter ب	As on No. 133, but date ١٢٢٥
		There are numerous variations in the date, and the same special marks occur as on the last coin.	
135 M	1226	As on No. 133, but letter ت	As on No. 133, but date ١٢٢٦
		Variations in the date, and special marks also occur.	
136	—	Elephant advancing to left with uplifted tail: above the tail a blundered date ١٢٢٣	پتن ضرب
		Traces of a lined circle and dots.	Field with dotted rosettes. Traces of a lined circle and dots.
137 M	—	Elephant advancing to right with uplifted tail. No date. In a double-lined circle with a row of dots.	As on No. 116.
		This coin is also found with a plain reverse.	
138	—	Elephant advancing to left with uplifted tail. No date. In a double-lined circle with a row of dots.	As on No. 116.
		HALF-PAISA.	
139 M	1200	Elephant advancing to left with uplifted tail: above the tail the date ١٢٠٠	پتن ضرب
		In a double-lined circle with a row of dots.	On a field with dotted rosettes. In a double-lined circle with a row of dots.
140 M	1201	As on No. 139, but date ١٢٠١ Pl. III.	As on No. 139.

PATTAN.

Metal. Number.	Date.	Obverse.	Reverse.
		HALF-PAISA—*cont.*	
Æ 141	1215	As on No. 139, but date ١٢١٥ Pl. III.	As on No. 139.
142 M	"	As on No. 139, but date ١٢١٤ and last two figures to left of the tail. Pl. III.	Do.
143 M	1216	As on No. 139, but date ١٢١٦	Do.
		There is a larger and thinner variety with the diameter of the inner circle 15·5 mm., and a smaller thicker variety with the corresponding diameter 14 mm.	
144 M	1217	As on No. 139, but date ١٢١٧ and last figure to left of the tail.	پتن ضرب On a field with dotted rosettes. In a double-lined circle with a row of dots.
145 M	1218	As on No. 139, but date ١٢١٨	As on No. 144.
146 M	1219	As on No. 139, but date ١٢١٩	Do.
		There is a variety with the reverse-field plain.	
147 M	1220	As on No. 139, but date ١٢٢٠	As on No. 144.
		From one to three figures of the date may be placed to left of the elephant's tail, and the reverse field may be plain.	
148 M	"	Elephant advancing to right with uplifted tail: above the elephant the date ١٢٢٠ In a double-lined circle with a row of dots. Pl. III.	As on No. 144, but the field plain.
		A variety occurs with dotted rosettes on the reverse.	

PATTAN.

Metal. Number.	Date.	Obverse.	Reverse.
		HALF-PAISA—*cont.*	
Æ 149 M	1221	As on No. 139, but date ١٢٢١ and three figures to left of the tail.	As on No. 144.
		A variety occurs with a plain reverse.	
150 M	,,	As on No. 148, but date ١٢٢١	As on No. 148.
151 M	,,	As on No. 150. Pl. III.	بهرام پتن ضرب A dotted rosette on the field. In a double-lined circle with a row of dots.
152 M	1222	As on No 148, but date ١٢٢٢	As on No. 148.
153 M	,,	As on No. 139, but date ١٢٢٢	بهرام ضرب پتن On a plain field. In a double-lined circle with a row of dots.
		From one to three figures of the date may be placed to left of the elephant's tail.	
154 M	,,	As on No. 148, but date ١٢٢٢	As on No. 151.
155	,,	As on No. 154.	As on No. 153, but a dotted rosette in the upper part of the field.
156 M	1223	As on No. 148, but date ١٢٢٣	As on No. 148.
157 M	,,	As on No. 139, but date ١٢٢٣ and last figure to left of the elephant's tail.	As on No. 153. Pl. IV.

PATTAN.

Metal. Number.	Date.	Obverse.	Reverse.
		HALF-PAISA—*cont.*	
Æ 158 M	1223	As on No. 156.	بهرام / ب / ضرب پٹن A dotted rosette in the upper part of the field. In a double-lined circle with a row of dots.
		There is a variety with a plain reverse.	
159 M	1224	Elephant advancing to right with depressed tail: above it the letter ا In a double-lined circle with a row of dots. Pl. IV.	بهرام ١٢٢٤ / ضرب / پٹن In a double-lined circle with a row of dots.
		Variations in the position of the figures of the date are met with, the most striking being one in which the first two figures are to right of the letters ام of بهرام. In some examples the reverse shows dotted rosettes, or a four-pointed star, and I have seen one in which the reverse inscription was hopelessly blundered and the date inverted.	
160 M	1225	As on No. 159, but letter ب	As on No. 159, but date ١٢٢٥
		In some examples dotted rosettes are found on the reverse. The chief variations in the date are:—(*a*) numeral ١ to right of ام of بهرام, (*b*) numerals ٢١ to right of ام (*c*). numeral ٥ much larger than the other three.	
161 M	1226	As on No. 159, but letter ت Pl. IV.	As on No. 159, but the date ١٢٢٦ placed in the right upper part of the field.
162	—	Elephant advancing to right with uplifted tail. No date. In a double-lined circle with a row of dots. Pl. IV.	As on No. 148.

PATTAN.

Metal. Number.	Date.	Obverse.	Reverse.
		HALF-PAISA—*cont.*	
Æ 163	—	Elephant advancing to left with uplifted tail. No date. In a double-lined circle with a row of dots.	As on No. 144.
		QUARTER-PAISA.	
164	1198	Elephant advancing to right. In a lined circle. *(Jackson.)*	ضرب پتن ۱۱۹۸
165 M	1200	Elephant advancing to left with uplifted tail: above the tail the date ۱۲۰۰ In a double-lined circle with a row of dots. Pl. IV.	پتن ب ضر On a field with dotted rosettes. In a double-lined circle with a row of dots.
166	1201	As on No. 165, but date ۱۲۰۱ Pl. IV.	As on No. 165.
167 M	1215	As on No. 165, but date ۱۲۱۵	Do.
168 M	"	As on No. 165, but date ۵۱۲۱	Do.
169 M	1216	As on No. 165, but date ٦۱۲۱	Do.

There is a larger and thinner coin with the diameter of the inner circle 11·5 mm., and a smaller and thicker one with the diameter 10 mm.

Metal. Number.	Date.	Obverse.	Reverse.
170 M	1217	As on No. 165, but date ۷۱۲۱	As on No. 165.
171 M	1218	As on No. 165, but date ۸۱۲۱	Do.

Weyl records this coin with the date written from left to right ۱۲۱۸, but this is probably an error, as he does not catalogue the normal type.

PATTAN.

QUARTER-PAISA—*cont.*

Metal. Number.	Date.	Obverse.	Reverse.
Æ 172	1219	As on No. 165, but date ٩١٢١	As on No. 165.
173	„	As on No. 172.	بهرام ضرب پتن

This coin with the designation بهرام in error for اختر is recorded by Jackson, who states that a specimen existed in the collection of Hultzsch.

Metal. Number.	Date.	Obverse.	Reverse.
174	1220	As on No. 165, but date ١٢٢٠	As on No. 165.

(Weyl.)

Metal. Number.	Date.	Obverse.	Reverse.
175 M	1221	As on No. 165, but date ١٢٢١ Pl. IV.	As on No. 165, but the field plain.

Jackson mentions a variety of this coin in which the date is represented only by the figures ١٢

Metal. Number.	Date.	Obverse.	Reverse.
176	„	Elephant advancing to right with uplifted tail: above the elephant the date ١٢٢١ In a double-lined circle with a row of dots. Pl. IV.	As on No. 175.
177	„	As on No. 176.	اختر ضرب پتن In a double-lined circle with a row of dots.
178 M	1222	As on No. 175, but date ٢٢٢١	As on No. 175.
179	„	As on No. 176, but date ٢٢٢١	Do.

PATTAN.

Metal. Number.	Date.	Obverse.	Reverse.
		QUARTER-PAISA—*cont.*	
Æ 180 M	1222	As on No. 178. **Pl. IV.**	اختر ب ضرب پتن In a double-lined circle with a row of dots.
181	1223	As on No. 165, but date ۳۲۲۱	As on No. 165.
		(Tufnell.)	
182 M	„	As on No. 176, but date ۳۲۲۱	As on No. 175.
183	„	As on No. 182. **Pl. IV.**	As on No. 177, but a four-dotted rosette below the word اختر
184	„	As on No. 181. **Pl. IV.**	As on No. 177.
185 M	1224	Elephant advancing to right with depressed tail: above it the letter ا In a double-lined circle with a row of dots.	اختر ۴۲۲۱ ب ضرب پتن In a double-lined circle with a row of dots.
		Variations occur with regard to the figures of the date, in the most striking of which the last numeral is placed below the word اختر (Jackson, pl. II, 439).	
186 M	1225	As on No. 185, but letter ب **Pl. IV.**	As on No. 185, but date ٥۲۲۱
		Similar variations to those of No. 185 occur also in this coin, including the one with the last numeral of the date placed below the word اختر. In another the entire date, which is incorrectly given as ۴۲۲۱, is placed below the same word.	

PATTAN.

Metal. Number.	Date	Obverse.	Reverse.
		QUARTER-PAISA—*cont.*	
Æ 187 M	1226	As on No. 185, but letter ت Pl. IV.	As on No. 185, but date ٦٢٢١
		There are numerous variations in the arrangement of the numerals of the date, the most noteworthy being:—(*a*) last figure below the ب of ضرب (*b*) last figure below the word اختر (*c*) entire date below this word.	
188 M	—	Elephant advancing to right with uplifted tail. No date. In a double-lined circle with a row of dots. Pl. IV.	پتن ضرب On a plain field. In a double-lined circle with a row of dots.
		EIGHTH-PAISA.	
189	1216	Elephant advancing to left with uplifted tail: above the elephant the date ٦١٢١ In a double-lined circle with a row of dots.	پتن ضرب On a plain field. In a double-lined circle with a row of dots.
		(Jackson.)	
190	1217	As on No. 189, but date ٧١٢١ *(Jackson.)*	As on No. 189.
191 M	1218	As on No. 189, but date ٨١٢١ Pl. IV.	Do.
192	1221	As on No. 189, but date ١٢٢١	Do.
193	1222	As on No. 189, but date ٢٢٢١	قطب ضرب In a double-lined circle with a row of dots.
		No mint-town is recorded on this coin, hence it may have been issued from some other mint than Pattan. It was first recorded by Hultzsch and is figured by Jackson (Pl. II, 405).	

PATTAN.

Metal. Number.	Date.	Obverse.	Reverse.
		EIGHTH-PAISA—*cont.*	
Æ 194	1222	Elephant advancing to right with uplifted tail: above the elephant the date ١٢٢٢ In a double-lined circle with a row of dots. Pl. IV.	قطب پتن ضرب On a field with dotted rosettes. In a double-lined circle with a row of dots.
195	1224	Elephant advancing to right with depressed tail: above the elephant the letter ا In a double-lined circle with a row of dots. Pl. IV.	١٢٢٤ قطب ب ضر پتن On a plain field. In a double-lined circle with a row of dots.
196	1225	As on No. 195, but letter ب	As on No. 195, but date ١٢٢٥
197	1226	As on No. 195, but letter ت	As on No. 195, but date ١٢٢٦
		In the only example of this coin that I have seen, in the collection of the British Museum, the first two numerals of the date are placed above the letter ب of قطب while the last two numerals are below the same letter. Neumann (pl. 79, 39129) gives a figure of the coin without a date, but this is perhaps an error of omission on the part of his draughtsman.	
198	—	Elephant advancing to right with uplifted tail. No date. In a double-lined circle with a row of dots.	پتن ضرب On a plain field. In a double-lined circle with a row of dots.

2. NAGAR نگر

(The City.)

This town, in the Shimoga district of Mysore, which is situated in the north-west corner of the State, was formerly, under the name of Bednūr, capital of the country ruled by the Ikkēri chiefs. The last Rājā of Bednūr died in 1755, leaving an adopted son as his heir, and the town was taken by Haidar Alī in March 1763, when the Rāni and adopted heir were both imprisoned. Bednūr was the most important of Haidar's annexations, and he always considered that its capture led the way to his ultimate success. He renamed the town Haidarnagar after himself, and intended to make it his capital; it became his family residence, and he established a local mint, where the well-known Haidarī pagodas and fanams were struck, and according to Rāmchāndra Rao (*Memoirs of Haidar Ali Bahadur and of his son Tippoo Sultan*) also rupees.* Nagar surrendered to General Matthews in January 1783, but was retaken by Tīpū Sultān about three months later, when the entire British garrison capitulated, and since this time it has remained in Mysore.

From the Nagar mint, and in this respect it stands alone among Tīpū's mints, were issued coins from the first regnal year to the last, without a break. The series includes in gold a single ahmadī, several pagodas of both the earlier and later (fārūqī) types, and a number of fanams; in silver there is a small set of double-rupees, rupees, and a half-rupee, while all the copper denominations, from the double-paisa to the eighth-paisa, are met with. A paisa and half-paisa dated 1227, are the only coins known to have been issued in the last year of Tīpū's reign, which commenced less than a month before his death, and no doubt their occurrence is explained by the remoteness of Nagar from the area of the military operations which culminated in the final capture of Seringapatam. In all the coins the border consists of a single or double-lined circle with a row of dots.

Special attention may be drawn to Nos. 251, 252, 254, 255 (two paisas of 1225 and two of 1226) which bear incorrect dates on the obverse. There is also a quarter-paisa dated 1261, probably in error for 1221, and in three quarter-paisas of 1221 and 1226, two of which bear blundered dates on the obverse, the designation *zohrā* (paisa) is found in place of the correct term *akhtar*. In my opinion this is the result of an error on the part of the die-engraver, rather than a deliberate attempt to enhance the value of the coin.

The gold ahmadī is of great rarity, but some of the pagodas and fanams are not uncommon. All the silver coins are of considerable rarity, the rupees being, however, more frequently met with than the other values. Of the copper coins the double-paisas are all rare, and the one-eighth paisa extremely rare; many of the paisas and half-paisas are still commonly found, but none of the quarter-paisas is common. While a number of the paisas struck before 1220 are not uncommon, those issued after

---

* As rupees struck by Haidar are not known to numismatists this statement is probably incorrect.

this year are found in still greater numbers, and the same statement applies to the half-paisas, which are, however, less common than the paisas. The following copper coins are all of considerable rarity :—Nos. 231, 244, 251, 252, 254, 255, 260, 264, 270, 278, 279, 283, 284.

NAGAR.

Metal. Number.	Date.	Obverse.	Reverse.
		AHMADI.	
AV *199	1216	محمد احمد دين درجهان است ح ضرب روشن زفتح حيدر احمد ٦١٢١ نگر سال مارا سنه *(Jackson).*	هو الو السلطان حيد تاريخ سال سخ العادل جلوس مـ ٦ ميوم بهاري سنه جلو
		PAGODA.	
200 M	1198	ح نگر On a granulated field : in a double-lined circle with a row of dots. Pl. IV.	هو ن السلطا ١١٩٨ هجر العادل سنه In a double-lined circle with a row of dots.
201 M	1199	As on No. 200, but regnal year ٣	As on No. 200, but date ١١٩٩
202 M	1200	As on No. 200, but regnal year ۴	As on No. 200, but date ١٢٠٠
203 M	1215	As on No. 200, but regnal year ٥	هو محمد السلطان العا ٥١٢١ دل سنه In a double-lined circle with a row of dots.

* I have not seen this coin, and have assumed that the inscriptions are similar to those on the contemporaneous ahmadis of Pattan.

NAGAR.

Metal. Number.	Date.	Obverse.	Reverse.
		PAGODA—*cont.*	
AI 204 M	1216	فاروق ٦ نگر ح سنہ In a double-lined circle with a row of dots. Pl. IV.	هو محمد السلطان حيـــد ٦١٢١ الو العادل سنہ In a double-lined circle with a row of dots.
205	1217	As on No. 204, but regnal year ٧	As on No. 204, but date ٧١٢١
		FANAM.	
206	1197	ح On a plain field : in a lined circle with a row of dots.	١١٩٧ لـــب ضرلگر In a lined circle with a row of dots.
207 M	1198	As on No. 206. Pl. IV.	As on No. 206, but date ١١٩٨
208 M	1199	Do.	Do. do. ١١٩٩
209 M	1200	Do.	Do. do. ١٢٠٠
210	1215	Do.	Do. do. ١٢١٥
211	,,	Do.	Do. do. ٥١٢١
212 M	1216	Do.	Do. do. ٦١٢١
213 M	1217	Do.	Do. do. ٧١٢١
214 M	1220	Do. Pl. IV.	Do. do. ٠٢٢١
215	1221	Do.	Do. do. ١٢٢١

The reverse field may have one or two dotted rosettes, or they may be absent.

NAGAR.

DOUBLE-RUPEE.

Metal. Number.	Date.	Obverse.	Reverse.
AR 216	1200	احمد دین در جهان است ح ضرب نگر روشن زفتح حیدر ۱۲۰۰ سال داو سنه هجر On a field ornamented with dotted rosettes : in a lined circle with a row of dots.	هو السلطان حید آلو العادل سیوم بهار ع سال داو سنه جلوس On a field ornamented with dotted rosettes : in a lined circle with a row of dots.

(*Taylor, pl. II, fig. 10.*)

Metal. Number.	Date.	Obverse.	Reverse.
217	1215	احمد محمد دین در جهان است ح روشن زفتح حیدر ۱۲۱۵ ضر نگر سال شا سنه On a field ornamented with dotted rosettes : in a double-lined circle with a row of dots.	As on No. 216, but cyclic year شا and regnal year ٥ On a field ornamented with dotted rosettes : in a double-lined circle with a row of dots.

(*Marsden, pl. XLV, fig. dccccxciv.*)

RUPEE.

Metal. Number.	Date.	Obverse.	Reverse.
218	1200	As on No. 216.	As on No. 216.

NAGAR.

Metal. Number.	Date.	Obverse.	Reverse.
		RUPEE—*cont.*	
AR 219 M	1216	احمد محمد دين در جهان روشن امـــــــــت زفتح حيدر امام ضرب ٦١٢١ نگر سال مارا سنه On a field ornamented with dotted rosettes : in a double-lined circle with a row of dots. Pl. IV.	هو السلطان الو العادل حيـــــــــد تاريخ جلوس سال سخ سيوم بهار سنه ٦ جلوس On a field ornamented with dotted rosettes : in a double-lined circle with a row of dots.
		HALF-RUPEE.	
220	1215	As on No. 217.	As on No. 217.
		DOUBLE-PAISA.	
Æ 221 M	1218	Elephant advancing to right with trunk uplifted, date ٨١٢١ over the tail which is depressed : above the elephant a flag, with a star in a central square surrounded by a border of dashes. In a double-lined circle with a row of dots. Pl. IV.	عثماني نگر ضرب دارالسلطنت On a field with dotted rosettes : in a double-lined circle with a row of dots.
222	1222	Elephant advancing to left with trunk uplifted, date ٢٢٢١ over the tail which is depressed : above the elephant a flag, with a star in a central square surrounded by a border of dashes. In a double-lined circle with a row of dots.	مشتري نگر ضرب دارالسلطنت On a field with dotted rosettes : in a double-lined circle with a row of dots.

Metal. Number.	Date.	Obverse.	Reverse.
		DOUBLE-PAISA—*cont.*	
Æ 223 M	1223	As on No. 222, but date ٣٢٢١ Pl. IV.	As on No. 222.
224	1224	Elephant advancing to right with trunk and tail both depressed: above the elephant a flag, with the letter ا and four oblique dashes passing to the angles of the flag. In a double-lined circle with a row of dots. Pl. V.	مشتري نگر ب ضرب ١٢٢٤ مولودي سنه On a field with dotted rosettes: in a double-lined circle with a row of dots.
225 M	1225	As on No. 224, but the letter ب on the flag.	As on No. 224, but date ٥٢٢١
226	1226	As on No. 224, but the letter ت on the flag. Pl. V.	As on No. 224, but date ٦٢٢١
227	—	As on No. 221, but without date.	As on No. 221.
		PAISA.	
228 M	1197	Elephant advancing to right with uplifted tail. In a double-lined circle with a row of dots. Pl. v.	١١٩٧ نگر سنه ضرب On a field with dotted rosettes: in a double-lined circle with a row of dots.
		In some examples there is a dotted rosette above the elephant's head.	
229 M	1199	As on No. 228.	١١٩٩ ب ضرنگر On a field with dotted rosettes: in a double-lined circle with a row of dots.

NAGAR.

Metal. Number.	Date.	Obverse.	Reverse.
		PAISA—*cont.*	
Æ 230 M	1200	Elephant advancing to right with uplifted tail: date ١٢٠٠ above the tail. In a double-lined circle (without dots). Pl. V.	نگر ضرب On a field with dotted rosettes: in a double-lined circle with a row of dots.
231	1201	As on No. 230, but date ١٢٠١	As on No. 230.
		(Moor, pl. II, fig. 7.)	
232 M	1215	As on No. 230, but date ١٢١٥	Do.
233 M	1216	As on No. 230, but date ١٢١٦	Do.
234 M	„	Elephant advancing to left with uplifted tail: date ١٢١٦ above the tail. In a double-lined circle (without dots).	Do.
235 M	1217	As on No. 234, but date ١٢١٧ Pl. V.	Do.
236 M	1218	As on No. 234, but date ١٢١٨	Do.
237 M	1219	As on No. 234, but date ١٢١٩	Do.
238 M	1220	As on No. 234, but date ١٢٢٠	Do.
239 M	1221	As on No. 234, but date ١٢٢١	Do.
240	„	As on No. 239.	زهرا ضرب ضر نگر On a field with dotted rosettes: in a double-lined circle with a row of dots.

NAGAR.

Metal. Number.	Date.	Obverse.	Reverse.
		PAISA—*cont*	
Æ 241	1221	As on No. 234, but ١٢٢١ مولودي above the elephant.	As on No. 240.
		(Jackson.)	
242 M	1222	As on No. 234, but date ١٢٢٢, and the elephant's tail depressed. Pl. V.	Do.
243 M	1223	As on No. 242, but date ١٢٢٣	Do.
244 M	,,	Elephant advancing to right with uplifted tail: date ١٢٢٣ above the elephant. In a double-lined circle with a row of dots.	As on No. 230.
245	,,	As on No. 244.	As on No. 240.
		(Jackson.)	
246	,,	As on No. 242, but ١٢٢٣ مولودي above the elephant.	Do.
		(Jackson.)	
247 M	1224	Elephant advancing to left with tail depressed: above the elephant's back the letter ا and date ١٢٢٤ to right of field. In a double-lined circle.	Do.
248		As on No. 247.	As on No. 230.
		(Jackson.)	

NAGAR.

PAISA—*cont.*

Metal. Number.	Date.	Obverse.	Reverse.
Æ 249 M	1224	Elephant advancing to right with tail depressed: above the elephant's back the letter ا In a double-lined circle with a row of dots. Pl. V.	زهرا نگر ضرب ۴۲۲۱ سنه مولودي In a double-lined circle with a row of dots.
		The ضر of ضرب is sometimes placed vertically on the extreme right of the field.	
250 M	1225	As on No. 249, but letter ب	As on No. 249, but date ۵۲۲۱
251 M	"	Elephant advancing to right with uplifted tail: above the elephant's tail the figures ٦١٢ (in error for ۵۲۲۱) Border doubtful. Pl. V.	As on No. 250.
252 M	"	As on No. 244, with date ۳۲۲۱ (in error for ۵۲۲۱) Pl. V.	Do.
253 M	1226	As on No. 249, but letter ت	As on No. 249, but date ٦٢٢۱
254	"	As on No. 251 (with figures ٦١٢) In a double-lined circle with a row of dots.	As on No. 253, but date represented by figures ٦٢٢ and the inscription roughly executed.
255	"	As on No. 254. Pl. V.	As on No. 230.
		This may possibly be a coin of 1216, but the obverse and its association with the reverses of coins dated 1225 and 1226 suggest a later period.	

NAGAR.

Metal. Number.	Date.	Obverse.	Reverse.
		PAISA—*cont.*	
Æ 256 M	1227	As on No. 249, but letter ث	As on No. 249, but date ۱۲۲۷
257	—	Elephant advancing to left with tail uplifted. No date. Border doubtful.	As on No. 230.
258	—	Elephant advancing to right with tail uplifted. No date. In a double-lined circle with a row of dots.	Do.
		HALF-PAISA.	
259 M	1200	Elephant advancing to right with tail uplifted: above the tail the date ۱۲۰۰ In a double-lined circle. Pl. v.	نگر ضرب On a field with dotted rosettes: in a double-lined circle with a row of dots.
260	1201	As on No. 259, but date ۱۲۰۱	As on No. 259.
		(Jackson.)	
261 M	1215	As on No. 259, but date ۱۲۱۵	Do.
262 M	1216	Elephant advancing to left with tail uplifted: above the tail the date ۱۲۱۶ In a double-lined circle.	Do.
263 M	1217	As on No. 262, but date ۱۲۱۷	Do.
264 M	1221	As on No. 262, but date ۱۲۲۱	Do.

NAGAR.

Metal. Number.	Date.	Obverse.	Reverse.
		HALF-PAISA—*cont.*	
Æ 265 M	1222	As on No. 262, but date ١٢٢٢ Pl. v.	بهرام ب ضر نگر On a field with dotted rosettes: in a double-lined circle with a row of dots.
266 M	1223	As on No. 262, but date ١٢٢٣	As on No. 265.
267 M	1224	As on No. 262, but letter ا above the elephant and date ١٢٢٤ to right of field.	Do.
268 M	1225	Elephant advancing to right with tail depressed: above the elephant's back the letter ب In a double-lined circle with a row of dots.	بهرام نگر ضرب ١٢٢٥ مولودے On a plain field, in a double-lined circle with a row of dots.
269 M	1226	As on No. 268, but letter ت	As on No. 268, but date ١٢٢٦
270 M	1227	As on No. 268, but letter ث Pl. vi.	As on No. 268, but date ١٢٢٧
271	—	Elephant advancing to left. No date. In a double-lined circle.	As on No. 259.

(Jackson.)

NAGAR.

Metal. Number.	Date.	Obverse.	Reverse.
		QUARTER-PAISA.	
Æ 272	1198	Elephant advancing to right with uplifted tail, and right front-foot raised. In a lined circle with a row of dots. Pl. VI.	١١٩٨ نگر منہ ضرب In a lined circle with a row of dots.
273 M	1200	Elephant advancing to right with uplifted tail: above the tail the date ١٢٠٠ In a double-lined circle.	نگر ضرب On a field with dotted rosettes: in a double-lined circle with a row of dots.
274 M	1216	As on No. 273, but date ٦١٢١ *(Tufnell.)*	As on No. 273.
275	"	Elephant advancing to left with uplifted tail: above the tail the date ٦١٢١ In a double-lined circle.	Do. Pl. VI.
276	1217	As on No. 273, but date ٧١٢١ *(Tufnell.)*	Do.
277	"	As on No. 275, but date ٧١٢١ *(Jackson.)*	Do.
278	1221	As on No. 273, but date ١٩٢١ (probably in error for ١٢٢١) *(Weyl, No. 3724.)*	زهرا ب ضر نگر (The word زهرا in error for اختر) In a double-lined circle with a row of dots.

NAGAR.

Metal. Number.	Date.	Obverse.	Reverse.
		QUARTER-PAISA—*cont.*	
Æ 279	1224	Elephant advancing to right with tail depressed: above the elephant's back the letter ا In a double-lined circle with a row of dots.	اختر نگر ضرب ۱۲۲۴ In a double-lined circle with a row of dots.
		(Schulman: White-King Catalogue.)	
280	„	Elephant advancing to left with uplifted tail: above the elephant the letter ا and to right of field the date ۱۲۲۴ In a double-lined circle.	اختر نگر ضرب On a field with dotted rosettes. In a double-lined circle with a row of dots.
		(Report, Mysore Arch. Survey, 1912–13, pl. IX, fig. 43.)	
281 M	1225	As on No. 279, but letter ب	As on No. 279, but date ۱۲۲۵
282 M	1226	As on No. 279, but letter ت Pl. VI.	As on No. 279, but date ۱۲۲۶
283	„	Elephant advancing to right with uplifted tail: above the elephant the date ۱۲۱۱ (in error for ۱۲۲۶) In a double-lined circle with a row of dots. Pl. VI.	As on No. 282, but word زهرا (in error for اختر).
284	—	As on No. 283, but without date.	As on No. 283.

NAGAR.

Metal. Number.	Date.	Obverse.	Reverse.
		EIGHTH-PAISA.	
Æ 285 M	1226	Elephant advancing to right with tail depressed: above the elephant the letter ت In a lined circle with a row of dots. Pl. VI.	قطب ضرب نگر ۱۲۲۶ In a double-lined circle with a row of dots.

3. FAIZ HISĀR, فيض حصار

(The Fort of Bounty).

This name was applied to Gooty, an important town in the Anantapūr district, with a very strong hill-fort which rises about 1,000 feet above the surrounding country. Marsden makes the title the equivalent of 'the fort of abundance,' while Taylor who follows Bowring (*Rulers of India, Tipū Sultān*, p. 210) prefers 'the citadel of grace.' Gooty came under the dominion of the Marāthās in 1758, and was taken by Haidar Alī from the celebrated Morāri Rāo in 1775, after a siege of nine months. The upper fort was practically impregnable, but it is said that the failure of a spring of water on which the garrison depended, led to the final capitulation. The town remained in possession of Tīpū till 1799, when it was captured by General Bowser. After the death of Tīpū Gooty was restored to the Nizām, in whose territory it was included before the Marāthā invasion, but in 1800, Anantapūr along with the Bellary and Cuddapah districts, was ceded to the East India Company.

The coins of this mint consist of an extensive series of paisas, half-paisas and quarter-paisas, issued from 1215 to 1226. On many of them the inscriptions are coarsely executed, and there are frequent blunders in the dates, due to misplaced or reversed numerals, and errors in the denomination of the coins. The three latest paisas bear the denomination *zohra*, and the letters ا ب and ت; as they also bear dates which are usually blundered, the safest course to adopt is to suppose that these letters, as in the Seringapatam and Nagar series, stand respectively for the years 1224, 1225 and 1226, and to date the coins accordingly. Unlike most of the letter coins of the two mints just referred to, those of Faiz Hisār are frequently dated on the obverse, but the date in a good many cases does not agree with that of the letter year, and in No. 339 different dates are found on the obverse and reverse, neither of which agrees with that of the letter. Fewer errors are met with in the half-paisas, and those of the last three years bear the denomination *bahrām* and the same letters as the paisas. Considerable difficulties are encountered in the later quarter-paisas, where in addition to numerous date errors there are also errors in the denomination of the coin. Thus in place of the correct term *akhtar*, quarter-paisas of the years 1225 and 1226 bear the designation *bahrām* (half-paisa), and one of 1225 is actually inscribed *zohra* (paisa). As we have already mentioned, Tīpū occasionally allowed his coins to circulate at a higher value than they originally represented, and the suggestion has been made that the coins referred to in the last sentence were deliberately overvalued. It appears to me much more probable that they are ordinary errors, such as are frequently met with elsewhere among Tīpū's coins, and that they resulted from an imperfect knowledge of the Hindustani letters, on the part of the Telugu or other South Indian workmen who constructed the dies.

In one of the paisas of 1225, a peculiar oblique oval mark is met with, as on some of the Seringapatam coins, although the fact that the coin bears a blundered date hardly suggests that it was made at the latter mint. The same mark occurs on the half-paisas of 1225 and 1226, on a quarter-paisa of 1225, and on three quarter-paisas of 1226.

In the coins of 1215 and 1216, there is an ornamental border in the form of a wide double-lined circle enclosing groups of four-dotted flowers. Commencing with 1216, in which year both types of border occur, and continuing to the last year, the border consists of the usual double-lined circle enclosing a row of dots.

Gooty was the seat of a mint before it was occupied by Haidar and Tīpū, and gold pagodas were previously struck by the Marāthās in the name of Muhammad Shāh, in imitation of what are apparently true Mughal pagodas appearing first in the reign of Farrukh-Siyar. These 'old Muhammad Shāhi pagodas,' as they were termed, appear to have had an extensive local circulation, and were succeeded by the 'new Muhammad Shāhi pagodas' struck in the first place by Haidar, but continued by Tīpū. Two of these coins are recorded in this catalogue under the issues of Haidar, although one of them, which is there classified for convenience, must from its date have been struck during the reign of Tīpū. It was probably struck without Tīpū's knowledge, and as it does not conform to his general policy in regard to coins was perhaps soon suppressed.

Many of the coins of Faiz Hisār are still fairly common, more particularly the paisas of 1216 (with elephant to right), of 1217, 1221 and 1222, and the half-paisas of 1216 (both borders), 1217, 1218, 1221, 1222 and 1223; the later paisas and half-paisas from 1223 onwards, with the exception of No. 314, are all rare, yet several of the quarter-paisas of the same period are not uncommon. The quarter-paisas issued before 1222 are all rare.

FAIZ HISĀR.

Metal. Number.	Date.	Obverse.	Reverse.
		PAISA.	
Æ 286 M	1215	Elephant advancing to left with uplifted tail: above the elephant the date ١٢١٥ In a wide double-lined circle enclosing 4-dotted rosettes. Pl. VI.	حصار فيض ضرب On a field with dotted rosettes. In a wide double-lined circle enclosing 4-dotted rosettes.
287 M	1216	As on No. 286, but date ١٢١٦ and a double-lined border with a single row of dots. Pl. VI.	As on No. 286.

FAIZ ḤISĀR.

Metal. Number.	Date.	Obverse.	Reverse.
		PAISA—*cont.*	
Æ 288 M	1216	Elephant advancing to right with uplifted tail: above the tail the date ١٢١٦ In a double-lined circle with a row of dots.	حصار فيض ب ضرب On a field with dotted rosettes. In a double-lined circle with a row of dots.
289 M	1217	As on No. 288, but date ١٢١٧	As on No. 288.
290	1218	As on No. 288, but date ١٢١٨	Do.
291 M	„	Elephant advancing to left with uplifted tail: above the elephant's head the date ١٢١٨ In a double-lined circle with a row of dots. Pl. VI.	Do.
292	1220	As on No. 288, but date ١٢٠٢ (in error for ١٢٢٠)	Do.

(Hultzsch.)

Metal. Number.	Date.	Obverse.	Reverse.
293 M	1221	As on No. 288, but above the elephant's back the date ١٢٢١	Do.
294	„	As on No. 291, but above the elephant the date ١٢٢١	Do.

(Jackson.)

FAIZ HISĀR.

Metal. Number.	Date.	Obverse.	Reverse.
		PAISA—*cont.*	
Æ 295 M	1221	As on No. 288, but above the elephant the date ١٦٦١ (in error for ١٢٢١)	As on No. 288. Pl. VI.
296 M	1222	As on No. 288, but above the elephant the date ٢٢٢١	Do.
297	,,	As on No. 288, but above the elephant the date ١٢٢٢ Pl. VI.	Do.
298	,,	As on No. 291, but above the elephant the date ٢٢٢١	As on No. 288, but a plain field.
		(Jackson.)	
299 M	1224	Elephant advancing to right with tail depressed: above the elephant the letter ا In a double-lined circle with a row of dots. Pl. VI.	مولود ي زهره ضر ب فيض حصار ٤٢٢١ In a double-lined circle with a row of dots.
300	,,	As on No. 299.	As on No. 299, but date ٤٢١٢ (in error for ٤٢٢١) placed above the word مولودي
		(Jackson.)	
301 M	1225	As on No. 299, but above the elephant the letter ب and above this the date ٣٦٦١ (in error for ٥٢٢١) Pl. VI.	As on No. 299, but date ٣٦٦١ (in error for ٥٢٢١) placeda bove the word مولودي and a special pointed oval mark near the lower margin.

FAIZ HISĀR.

Metal. Number.	Date.	Obverse.	Reverse.
		PAISA—*cont.*	
Æ 302	1226	As on No. 299, but above the elephant the letter ت and the date ٦٢٢١	As on No. 299, but date ٦٢٢١
		(Jackson.)	
303	„	As on No. 302, but date ٢٢٢١ (in error for ٦٢٢١) above the letter.	As on No. 302.*
		(British Museum.)	
304	—	Elephant advancing to right. No date. In a double-lined circle.	As on No. 288.
		(Jackson.)	
		HALF-PAISA.	
305 M	1215	Elephant advancing to left with uplifted tail: above the elephant the date ٥١٢١ In a wide double-lined circle enclosing 4-dotted rosettes.	حصار فيض ضرب In a wide double-lined circle enclosing 4-dotted rosettes.
306 M	1216	As on No. 305, but date ٦١٢١	As on No. 305.
307 M	„	As on No. 306, but in a double-lined circle with a row of dots.	As on No. 306, but in a double-lined circle with a row of dots. A dotted rosette in the loop of the ض of فيض
308 M	1217	As on No. 307, but date ٧١٢١	As on No. 307.

* This is a conjecture, as in the only coin I have seen the reverse is almost illegible.

FAIZ HISĀR.

Metal, Number.	Date.	Obverse.	Reverse.
		HALF-PAISA—*cont.*	
Æ 309	1217	Elephant advancing to right with uplifted tail: above the elephant the date ٧١٢١ In a double-lined circle with a row of dots.	As on No. 307.
310 Æ	1218	As on No. 307, but date ٨١٢١ Pl. VI.	Do.
311 Æ	1221	As on No. 309, but date ١٢٢١	Do.
312 Æ	1222	As on No. 309, but date ٢٢٢١ Pl. VI.	Do.
313	„	As on No. 307, but date ٢٢٢١ *(Jackson.)*	Do.
314 Æ	1223	As on No. 309, but date ٣٢٢١	Do.
315 Æ	1224	Elephant advancing to right with uplifted tail: above the elephant the letter ا In a double-lined circle with a row of dots. Pl. VI.	١٢٢٤ ضرب بهرام فيض حصار In a double-lined circle with a row of dots.
316 Æ	1225	Elephant advancing to right with depressed tail: above the elephant the letter ب In a double-lined circle with a row of dots. Pl. VI.	٥٦٦١ بهرام ضرب فيض حصار Date ٥٦٦١ (in error for ٥٢٢١) Appointed oval mark near the lower margin. In a double-lined circle with a row of dots.

FAIZ HISĀR.

Metal. Number.	Date.	Obverse.	Reverse.
		HALF-PAISA—*cont.*	
Æ 317 M	1225	As on No. 316, but above the letter ب the date ٣٦٦١ (in error for ٥٢٢١)	As on No. 316, but date ٣٦٦١ (in error for ٥٢٢١) Pl. VI.
318 M	1226	As on No. 316, but above the elephant the letter ت and above this the date ٢٢٢١ (in error for ٦٢٢١) Pl. VI.	As on No. 316, but no date visible on the specimens examined.
319	—	Elephant advancing to right. No date. In a double-lined circle with a row of dots. *(Jackson.)*	As on No. 307.
		QUARTER-PAISA.	
320	1215	Elephant advancing to left with uplifted tail: above the elephant the date ٥١٢١ In a wide double-lined circle enclosing 4-dotted rosettes.	حصار فيض ب ضرب In a wide double-lined circle enclosing 4-dotted rosettes.
321	,,	As on No. 320, but date ١٢١٥ *(Jackson.)*	As on No. 320.
322 M	1216	As on No. 320, but date ٦١٢١ Pl. VI.	Do.
323	,,	As on No. 322. In a double-lined circle with a row of dots.	As on No. 320, but a dotted rosette in the loop of the ض of فيض In a double-lined circle with a row of dots.

FAIZ HISĀR.

Metal. Number.	Date.	Obverse.	Reverse.
		QUARTER-PAISA—*cont.*	
Æ 324	1217	As on No. 323, but date ٧١٢١	As on No. 323.
325	„	Elephant advancing to right with uplifted tail: above the elephant the date ٧١٢١ In a double-lined circle with a row of dots. *(Jackson.)*	Do.
326	1222	As on No. 325, but date ٢٢٢١	Do.
327	„	As on No. 325, but date ٦٢٢١ (in error for ٢٢٢١) *(Jackson.)*	Do.
328	„	As on No. 325, but date ٢٦٦١ (in error for ٢٢٢١)	Do
329	„	As on No. 326.	اختر ضرب فیض حصار In a double-lined circle with a row of dots.
330	1223	As on No. 325, but date ٣٢٢١	As on No. 323
331 M.	„	As on No. 325, but date ٣٦٦١ (in error for ٣٢٢١) and the elephant's tail depressed. Pl. VI.	Do.
332	„	As on No. 325, but date ٣١٦١ (in error for ٣٢٢١) Pl. VI.	Do.

FAIZ HISĀR.

Metal. Number.	Date.	Obverse.	Reverse.
		QUARTER-PAISA—*cont.*	
Æ 333	1224	Elephant advancing to right with depressed tail: above the elephant the letter ا In a double-lined circle with a row of dots.	۴۲۲۱ اختر ضرب فيض حصار In a double-lined circle with a row of dots.
334	1225	As on No. 333, but above the elephant the letter ب	As on No. 333, the date ۴۲۲۱ in error for ۵۲۲۱ In some specimens the date appears to be ۲۲۲۱
335	,,	As on No. 334.	As on No. 334, but value of coin زهره (in error for اختر)
		(Jackson.)	
336 M.	,,	Do. Pl. VII.	As on No. 333, but date ۲۲۲۱ (in error for ۵۲۲۱) and value of coin بهرام (in error for اختر)
337	,,	Do.	As on No. 336, but ضر of ضرب to right of field and a pointed oval mark near the lower margin.
338	,,	Do. Pl. VII.	As on No. 333, but date ۵۶۶۱ (in error for ۵۲۲۱) and value of coin بهرام (in error for اختر)
339	,,	As on No 334, but date ۲۲۲۱ (in error for ۵۲۲۱) above the letter.	As on No. 333, the date ۴۲۲۱ in error for ۵۲۲۱

FAIZ HISĀR.

Metal. Number.	Date.	Obverse	Reverse.
		QUARTER-PAISA—*cont.*	
Æ 340	1225	As on No. 339	As on No. 329.
341	,,	As on No. 334.	As on No. 323.
342 M.	1226	As on No. 333, but above the elephant the letter ت Pl. VII.	As on No. 329, but a pointed oval mark near the lower margin.
343	,,	As on No 342, but date ٦٢٢١ above the letter.	As on No. 329.
		(Tufnell.)	
344	,,	As on No. 343.	As on No. 329, but value of coin بہرام (in error for اختر)
345 M.	,,	As on No. 342, but date ٢٢٢١ (in error for ٦٢٢١) above the letter. Pl. VII.	As on No. 342.
		In some copies the two dots above the letter are omitted.	
346	,,	As on No. 342, but date ٦٦٦١ (in error for ٦٢٢١) above the letter.	Do.
		(Weyl.)	
347	?	Elephant advancing to right: above the elephant ٢.٢.٢.١	As on No. 329.
348	?	Elephant advancing to left with uplifted tail: above the elephant the figures ١٢٥ In a double-lined circle with a row of dots.	As on No. 320, but inscription blundered. In a double-lined circle with a row of dots.

FAIZ HISĀR.

Metal. Number.	Date.	Obverse.	Reverse.
		QUARTER-PAISA—*cont.*	
Æ 349	?	As on No. 348, but above the elephant the figures ۱۲ In a lined circle.	As on No. 348.
350	?	As on No. 348, but elephant's tail depressed and above the elephant ۹۱۵۱۷	Do.
351 M.	—	Elephant advancing to right No date. In a double-lined circle with a row of dots.	As on No. 320. In a double-lined circle with a row of dots.
		Jackson mentions a variety with a double-lined circle on the obverse not enclosing dots.	

4. BENGALŪR بنگلور

(Bengalūru, the City of Beans.)

Bangalore, the chief town of the district of the same name, is the largest city in Mysore State, and now includes an important British cantonment. It was long celebrated for its fort, which originally composed of earth was rebuilt in stone and greatly strengthened by Haider Alī, in the first year of his reign. Bangalore was a favourite residence of Tīpū, from whom it was taken by Lord Cornwallis on 21st March 1791, after a siege of seventeen days. The town was restored to Tīpū at the peace of 1792, when he dismantled the fort, but it was again rebuilt after his death, under the direction of Purnaiya, Dīwān of Krishnarājā.

Copper paisas, half-paisas, quarter-paisas and one-eighth paisas were struck at Bangalore between the fourth and ninth regnal years of Tīpū Sultān. The latest coins are dated 1219, a year which actually commenced fourteen days after the capture of Bangalore, but the town was restored to Tīpū by the treaty of Seringapatam, on 23rd February 1792, about a month before the close of 1219, and in all probability the coins of this year were issued during this period. Although Bangalore was held by Tīpū from 1792 to his death, all local coinage seems to have ceased after the year 1219, an apparent exception being the half-paisa dated 1222 (No. 370), which is more likely to be the result of some mixture of dies through error, than an evidence that coins were struck at Bangalore in the year recorded on this specimen. It is conceivable that in this case a discarded reverse die of Bangalore, got mixed up with a half-paisa obverse of Seringapatam or some other mint.

In all the coins of the Bangalore mint the inscription on the reverse is carefully executed, and the border on this side is the usual double-lined circle enclosing a row of dots. The elephant on the obverse is less satisfactory, and with the single exception of a half-paisa of 1215, in which the dots are present, is enclosed in a plain double-lined circle.

Several of the half-paisas and quarter-paisas of this mint are still commonly met with, but all the paisas and one-eighth paisas are more or less rare ; among the special rarities may be mentioned Nos. 363, 365, 370, 373 and 382. The coins of the first two years and of the last year are less common than those of the intermediate period.

BENGALŪR.

Metal. Number.	Date.	Obverse.	Reverse.
		PAISA.	
Æ 352 M	1200	Elephant advancing to right with uplifted tail: above the tail the date ١٢٠٠ In a double-lined circle.	بنگلور ضرب On a field ornamented with dotted rosettes. In a double-lined circle with a row of dots.
353 M	„	As on No. 352, but date ١٢١٠ (probably in error for ١٢٠٠) *.	As on No. 352.
354 M	1215	As on No. 352, but date ١٢١٥	Do.
355	„	As on No. 352, but date ٥١٢١	Do.
356 M	1216	As on No. 352, but date ١٢١٦ Pl. VII.	Do.
357	„	As on No. 352, but date ٠٢١٦ (in error for ١٢١٦)	Do.
358 M	1217	Elephant advancing to left with the tail bent forward over the back: above the tail the date ١٢١٧ In a double-lined circle.	Do. Pl. VII.
359 M	1218	As on No. 358, but date ٨١٢١	Do.
360	„	As on No. 352, but date ٨١٢١	Do.
		(Jackson.)	
361 M	1219	As on No. 358, but date ٩١٢١	Do.

* Moor records this coin as a paisa of 1210, but in his Pl. I, fig. 12, the date is wrongly shown as 1211.

BENGALŪR.

Metal. Number.	Date.	Obverse.	Reverse.
		HALF-PAISA.	
Æ 362 M	1215	Elephant advancing to right with uplifted tail: above the tail the date ١٢١٥ In a double-lined circle. Pl. VII.	بنگلور ضرب On a field ornamented with dotted rosettes. In a double-lined circle with a row of dots.
363 M	"	Elephant advancing to left with uplifted tail: above the tail the date ٥١٢١ In a double-lined circle with a row of dots.	As on No. 362.
364 M	1216	As on No. 362, but date ١٢١٦ Pl. VII.	Do.
365	"	As on No. 362, but date ٦١٢١ *(Jackson.)*	Do.
366 M	"	As on No. 363, but date ⁘١٢١ and a double-lined circle (without dots).	Do.
367 M	1217	As on No. 366, but date ٧ ١٢١	Do.
368 M	1218	As on No. 366, but date ٨١٢١ Pl. VII.	Do.
369 M	1219	As on No. 366, but date ٩١٢١	Do.
370 M	?	Elephant advancing to right with uplifted tail: above the elephant the date ٢٢٢١ In a double-lined circle with a row of dots. The date 1222 is an unlikely one for an issue of the Bengalūr mint. An obverse from some other mint has probably got mixed up with an older and discarded reverse from Bengalūr.	Do.

BENGALŪR.

Metal. Number.	Date.	Obverse.	Reverse.
		HALF-PAISA—*cont.*	
Æ 371	—	Elephant advancing to right No date. In a double-lined circle.	As on No. 362.
		(Tufnell.)	
		QUARTER-PAISA.	
372	1200	Elephant advancing to right with uplifted tail: above the tail the date ١٢٠٠ In a double-lined circle.	بنگلور ضرب On a field ornamented with dotted rosettes. In a double-lined circle with a row of dots.
373	„	As on No. 372, but date ١٢١٠ (in error for ١٢٠٠)	As on No. 372.
		*(Schulman : White-King Catalogue.)**	
374 M	1215	As on No. 372, but date ١٢١٥	Do.
375 M	1216	As on No. 372, but date ١٢١٦	Do.
376	„	As on No. 372, but date ٦١٢١	Do.
		(Jackson.)	
377	„	Elephant advancing to left with uplifted tail: above the tail the date ٦١٢١ In a double-lined circle.	Do.
378 M	1217	As on No. 377, but date ٧١٢١	Do.
379 M	1218	As on No. 377, but date ٨١٢١ Pl. VII.	Do.

* This coin, No. 5132 of the Catalogue, was described as of date 1221. Through the courtesy of M. Schulman I was able to examine it and found the date to be 1210, as described above.

BENGALŪR.

Metal. Number.	Date.	Obverse.	Reverse.
		QUARTER-PAISA—*cont.*	
Æ 380 M	1219	As on No. 377, but date ٩١٢١	As on No. 372.
381	—	As on No. 372, but no date.	Do.
		(Jackson.)	
		EIGHTH-PAISA.	
382	1216	Elephant advancing to right with uplifted tail: above the tail the date ٦١٢١ In a double-lined circle.	بنگلور ضرب On a field ornamented with dotted rosettes. In a double-lined circle with a row of dots.
		(Jackson.)	
383 M	1218	Elephant advancing to left with uplifted tail: above the tail the date ٨١٢١ In a double-lined circle.	As on No. 382. Pl. VII.
384	1219	As on No. 383, but date ٩١٢١	Do.

5. FARRUKH-YĀB HISĀR فرخياب حصار

(The fort felicitously acquired.)

This term was applied to Chitaldrūg, situated at the foot of a strongly fortified hill 126 miles north-west of Bangalore, and the chief town of the district of the same name in Mysore. The Poligar or local chief was forced to submit to Haidar Alī in 1762, but as he refused to assist his conqueror and had actually sided with the Marāthās and Nizām Alī in their operations against Mysore, the town was besieged and taken by Haidar in March 1779. The name selected by Tīpū possibly refers to the fact that the fort was captured through treachery, on the part of the Muhammadan officers in the army of the Poligar.

The mint-name has been read by Tufnell and others Farrukh-bāb Hisār, فرخباب حصار 'the fort of the fortunate gate,' but in the earlier coins the reading is undoubtedly ياب 'yab'. In the later coins the dots of the ي are misplaced, which has led to this letter being mistaken for a ب. Kirkpatrick (*Appendix E*, p. XLI), Captain Macleod (vide *Beatson, Appendix*, p. clxx) and Kirmani, all support the reading now adopted.

Copper coins of all the denominations were issued from this mint in the years 1215 to 1219, both included. Moor records and figures a paisa dated 1201, but as it has not been met with since his time it is possible that a coin of 1215 has been misread. Attention may be drawn to the two sizes of paisa issued in 1216. The coins of 1215 show a treble-lined border on both sides, while those of the later years have a double-lined circle enclosing a row of oblique dashes.

Many of the coins of this mint are still fairly common, in particular the half-paisas of 1217 and 1218; the coins of 1215 and 1219 are, however, less frequently met with than those of the other years. The double-paisas and one-eighth paisa are rare, and none of the quarter-paisas is common.

FARRUKH-YĀB HISĀR.

Metal. Number.	Date.	Obverse.	Reverse.
		DOUBLE-PAISA.	
Æ 385	1218	Elephant advancing to left with trunk upraised, date ٨١٢١ near the tail which is depressed: above the elephant a flag, with a star in a central square surrounded by a border of dashes. In a double-lined circle with a row of oblique dashes. Pl. VII.	عثماني فرخيا حصار ضرب دارالسلطنت On a field ornamented with dotted rosettes. In a double-lined circle with a row of oblique dashes.
386	1219	As on No. 385, but date ٩١٢١	As on No. 385.
		PAISA.	
387	1201	Elephant advancing to right with uplifted tail: above the elephant the date ١٢٠١ In a treble-lined circle.	فرخيا حصار ضرب On a field ornamented with dotted rosettes. In a treble-lined circle.
		(Moor, pl. II, fig. 8.)	
388	1215	As on No. 387, but date ١٢١٥	As on No. 387.
389 M	„	As on No. 387, but date ٥١٢١	Do.
390 M	„	As on No. 389.	فرخيا حصار ضرب On a field ornamented with dotted rosettes. In a treble-lined circle.
391 M	„	Elephant advancing to left with uplifted tail: above the elephant the date ٥١٢١ In a treble-lined circle.	As on No. 387. Pl. VII.

FARRUKH-YĀB HISĀR.

Metal. Number.	Date.	Obverse.	Reverse.
		PAISA—*cont.*	
Æ 392	1215	As on No. 391.	As on No. 390.
393 M	1216	As on No. 391, but date ١٢١٦: in a double-lined circle with a row of oblique dashes. Pl. VII.	As on No. 390, but ب of ضرب shorter. Two dotted rosettes near the upper margin. In a double-lined circle with a row of oblique dashes.
		Diameter of coin 21 mm., and of inner circle on obverse 16 mm.	
394	,,	As on No. 393. Pl. VII.	As on No. 393, but dotted rosettes on the field.
		Diameter of coin 25 mm., and of inner circle on obverse 19·5 mm.	
395 M	1217	As on No. 393, but date ١٢١٧	As on No. 394.
396 M	1218	As on No. 393, but date ١٢١٨	Do.
397 M	1219	As on No. 393, but date ١٢١٩	Do.
		HALF-PAISA.	
398 M	1215	Elephant advancing to right with uplifted tail: above the elephant the date ١٢١٥ In a treble-lined circle. Pl. VII.	فرخیا حصار ب ضرب On a field ornamented with dotted rosettes In a treble-lined circle.
399 M	1216	Elephant advancing to left with uplifted tail: above the elephant the date ١٢١٦ In a double-lined circle with a row of oblique dashes.	ب فرخیا حصار ضرب On a field ornamented with dotted rosettes. In a double-lined circle with a row of oblique dashes.

FARRUKH-YĀB HISĀR.

Metal. Number.	Date.	Obverse.	Reverse.
		HALF-PAISA—*cont.*	
Æ 400 M	1217	As on No. 399, but date ٧١٢١ Pl. VII.	As on No. 399.
401 M	1218	As on No. 399, but date ٨١٢١	Do.
402	1219	As on No. 399, but date ٩١٢١	Do.
		QUARTER-PAISA.	
403 M	1216	Elephant advancing to left with uplifted tail: above the elephant the date ٦١٢١ In a double-lined circle with a row of oblique dashes.	فرخيا حصار ضرب On a field ornamented with dotted rosettes. In a double-lined circle with a row of oblique dashes.
404 M	1217	As on No. 403, but date ٧١٢١ Pl. VII.	As on No. 403.
405	1218	As on No. 403, but date ٨١٢١	Do.
406	1219	As on No. 403, but date ٩١٢١	Do.
		EIGHTH-PAISA.	
407	1217	Elephant advancing to left with uplifted tail: above the elephant the date ٧١٢١ In a double-lined circle with a row of oblique dashes.	فرخيا حصا ضرب In a double-lined circle with a row of oblique dashes.

(*Report, Mysore Arch. Survey*, 1912-13, *pl. IX, fig.* 29.)

6. KALĪKŪT كليكوت

(Kolikod, cock-fort).

Calicut, the capital of the Malabar district, was taken by Haidar Alī in 1766 from the Zamorin or local ruler, who to evade capture allowed himself to be burned alive in his palace. Comparatively little was done to control the captured district, and the inhabitants led by the Nayar chiefs soon broke into revolt. In 1773 a force was sent by Haidar to Calicut, which quickly brought about the re-conquest of the whole of Malabar. The town was taken by a British army under Major Abington in 1782, but was restored to Tīpū Sultān later. Tīpū himself visited Malabar early in 1788 and made a stay of several months, during which arrangements were made for transferring the seat of government from Calicut to Feroke. Calicut was taken by British troops towards the close of 1790, and by the treaty of Seringapatam in 1792, the Malabar district came under the jurisdiction of the East India Company. The usual spelling of the mint-town is that given above, but on some of the coins it is Kalīkūṭ كليكوٹ .

Coins were struck at Calicut in gold, silver and copper, from the second to the fifth years of Tīpū's reign. The gold coins consist merely of fanams, which appeared in all the four years that the mint was active; the only silver coins known are two varieties of double-rupee struck in 1215, of which, judging from their present scarcity, the issue must have been very limited. The copper coins, so far as is known, consist only of paisas and quarter-paisas.

The oldest dated coin is a thick coarsely executed paisa of 1198, in which the name of the mint-town is to the right of the field, and some of the letters appear to be placed at right angles to those making up the rest of the inscription; in some examples the inscription has degenerated into a mere scrawl (*vide* Neumann, pl. 45, no. 20088). One of the words which Jackson reads سنه *sanah*, appears to me to be بندر *bundar*, a word which occurs clearly on another Calicut coin (No. 422). In the paisa of 1199, while the figure of the elephant is very crude, the inscription is more carefully executed. There is a variety of the last coin in which the elephant has a thinner body than usual, and extremely slender legs. The later paisas are all well made, and a feature of special interest is that the regnal year 4 is recorded on paisas of both 1200 and 1215. Very few instances are known of regnal years being recorded on the copper coins of Tīpū Sultān, this mode of reckoning being practically confined to the gold and silver issues. The undated paisa (No. 422) inscribed ضرب بندر كليكوٹ (struck at the port Kalīkūṭ), from its general appearance is probably an early coin. The quarter-paisas are all undated, and in some of them the inscriptions are very degenerate.

The gold and silver coins have the usual borders; while in the copper series may be found a pearled circle, a plain double-lined circle, or more commonly the usual double-lined circle enclosing a row of dots.

The gold fanams of Calicut are not uncommon, but as already indicated the silver double-rupees are of great rarity. None of the copper coins is now commonly met with, except perhaps the paisa of 1215 with the date reading from right to left. The undated paisa is extremely rare.

KALĪKŪT.

Metal. Number.	Date.	Obverse.	Reverse.
		FANAM.	
AV 408	1198	ح On a plain field: in a lined circle with a row of dots.	١١٩٨ سنه ت كليكو In a lined circle with a row of dots.
409 AV	1199	As on No. 408. Pl. VII.	As on No. 408, but date ١١٩٩
410 AV	1200	Do.	As on No. 408, but date ١٢٠٠
411 AV	1215	Do.	As on No. 408, but date ١٢١٥
412 AV	"	Do. Pl. VII.	As on No. 408, but date ٥١٢١
		DOUBLE-RUPEE.	
AR 413	1215	احمد دين درجهان است كليكوت ح روشن زفتح حيدر ضرب سال شا سنه ١٢١٥ محمد On a field ornamented with dotted rosettes: in a double-lined circle with a row of dots.	هو السلطان حيد الو العادل سيوم بهار ٥ سال شا سنه جلوس On a field ornamented with dotted rosettes: in a double-lined circle with a row of dots.

(*Taylor, pl. II, fig. 11.*)

KALĪKŪT.

Metal. Number.	Date.	Obverse.	Reverse

DOUBLE-RUPEE—*cont.*

Metal. Number.	Date.	Obverse.	Reverse
AR 414	1215	As on No. 413, but date ١٢١٥ and شا (name of the cyclic year) occupying the penultimate line.	As on No. 413.

(Schulman: White-King Catalogue, pl. I, No. 5099.)

PAISA.

Metal. Number.	Date.	Obverse.	Reverse
Æ 415 M	1198	Elephant advancing to right with uplifted tail. In a circle of large dots. Pl. VII.	كو ١١٩٨ بندر ضرب On a plain field: without marginal border.
416 M	1199	As on No. 415. Pl. VIII.	١١٩٩ كليكو ب ضر In a dotted circle.
417 M	1200	Elephant advancing to right with uplifted tail: above the elephant the date ١٢٠٠ In a double-lined circle. Pl. VII.	كليكوت ضرب On a field ornamented with dotted rosettes. In a double-lined circle with a row of dots.
		In some specimens the last letter ot the mint-name is ث	
418 M	"	As on No. 417. Pl. VIII.	كليكوث ب ضر سنه ع On a field ornamented with dotted rosettes. In a double-lined circle with a row of dots.

Metal. Number.	Date.	Obverse.	Reverse.
		PAISA—*cont.*	
Æ 419 M	1215	As on No. 417, but date ١٢١٥ : in a double-lined circle with a row of dots.	As on No. 418.
420 M	,,	As on No. 419. Pl. VIII.	كليكرت ضرب سنه ۴ A four-dotted rosette near the upper margin. In a double-lined circle with a row of dots.
421 M	,,	As on No. 419, but date ٥١٢١ * Pl. VIII.	As on No. 417.
		In same specimens the last letter of the mint-name is ث	
422 M	—	As on No. 415. Pl. VIII.	كليكوث بندر ضرب On a plain field: without marginal border.
		QUARTER-PAISA.	
423 M	—	Elephant to right with uplifted tail. In a dotted circle. Pl. VIII.	كليكو On a plain field: without marginal border.
424	—	As on No. 423. Pl. VIII.	ــتــ كليكو A dotted rosette to the left of the field. In a dotted circle.
425	--	Do.	A blundered inscription probably intended for كليكوت and below this two short vertical lines and two dots.

* Tufnell (pl. III, 152) figures a variety of this coin in which the right forefoot of the elephant is distinctly raised. The same writer records a paisa of 1218, but it appears out of place among the coins of 1215 in his catalogue, and the record is doubtless an error.

7. FARRUKHĪ فرخي

(Prosperity.)

This name was given to the place now known as Feroke, situated on the south bank of the Beypore River, about seven miles to the south of Calicut. In 1788, Tīpū Sultān, no doubt prompted by similar reasons to those which led to the destruction of the town of Mysore, demolished Calicut and commenced the erection of a fort a few miles away, around which in course of time it was hoped a new Calicut would arise. The fort was still unfinished on 10th December 1790, when it was taken by Colonel Hartley, after the defeat of Tīpū's army under Husain Alī. The designation of this mint is no more intelligible than are most of Tīpū's newly invented names, but in this case it has persisted to the present day, thus affording a solitary instance of the term which he adopted coming into general use.

The coins of this mint, which were issued during the years 1216, 1217 and 1218, consist of gold fanams, and in copper of a double-paisa, and single, half and quarter-paisas. Moor in his "*Narrative of the Operations of Little's Detachment*" (p. 475, pl. II, fig. 2), describes and figures a double-paisa of the year 1219, but there can be little doubt that he has misread a similar coin of the previous year, for the year 1219 actually commenced a few months after Farrukhī was captured by the British. Both Weyl and Jackson record a quarter-paisa dated 1226, doubtless a die error for 1216.

In the majority of the copper coins the ornamental border on both surfaces consists of the usual row of dots between two lined circles, but in two of the paisas of 1216 the dots are replaced by curved dashes.

The paisa of 1217 is still commonly found and that of the following year is not uncommon. The other coins are less frequently met with, the double-paisa, the paisas of 1216, and the quarter-paisas being all rare. The gold fanams are not uncommon.

FARRUKHĪ.

Metal. Number.	Date.	Obverse.	Reverse.
		FANAM.	
AV 426 M	1216	ح On a plain field: in a lined circle with a row of dots. Pl. VIII.	١٢١٦ فرخي In a lined circle with a row of dots.
427	1217	As on No. 426.	As on No. 426, but date ١٢١٧
428	1218	Do.	As on No. 426, but date ١٢١٨

FARRUKHĪ.

DOUBLE-PAISA.

Metal.	Number.	Date.	Obverse.	Reverse.
Æ	429 M	1218	Elephant advancing to right with uplifted trunk, date ١٢١٨ above the tail which is depressed: above the elephant a flag, with a star in a central square surrounded by a border of dashes. Margin ? * Pl. VIII.	عثماني فرخي ضرب دارالسلطنت On a plain field. Margin ?

PAISA.

Metal.	Number.	Date.	Obverse.	Reverse.
	430	1216	Elephant advancing to right with uplifted tail: above the elephant the word سنه and the date ١٢١٦ In a double-lined circle with a row of curved dashes.	فرخي ضرب On a field onamented with dotted rosettes. In a double-lined circle with a row of curved dashes.
			(British Museum.)	
	431	,,	As on No. 430, but word سنه omitted.	As on No. 430.
			(Tufnell.)	
	432	,,	As on No. 430, but in a double-lined circle with a row of dots.	As on No. 430, but in a double-lined circle with a row of dots.
			(Tufnell, pl. III, 169.)	
	433 M	1217	Elephant advancing to left with uplifted tail: above the elephant the date ١٢١٧ In a double-lined circle with a row of dots.	فرخي ضرب Three dotted rosettes in the lower part of the field. In a double-lined circle with a row of dots.

In some specimens the dotted rosettes are not confined to the lower part of the field.

* On all the specimens I have seen the marginal design was incomplete, but there were tracse of a lined circle, and the arrangement was probably the same as in the other coins of the Farrukhī mint.

FARRUKHĪ.

Metal. Number.	Date.	Obverse.	Reverse.
		PAISA—*cont.*	
Æ 434 M	1218	As on No. 433, but date ٨١٢١ Pl. VIII.	As on No. 433.
435 M	„	As on No. 434.	فرخي ضرب On a plain field. In a double-lined circle with a row of dots.
		HALF-PAISA.	
436 M	1217	Elephant advancing to left with uplifted tail: above the elephant the date ٧١٢١ In a double-lined circle with a row of dots. Pl. VIII.	فرخي ضرب Three dotted rosettes in the lower part of the field. In a double-lined circle with a row of dots.
437 M	1218	As on No. 436, but date ٨١٢١	As on No. 436.
		QUARTER-PAISA.	
438	1216	Elephant advancing to right with uplifted tail. Border?	٦٢٢١ سنه فرخي ضرب (Date ٦٢٢١ in error for ٦١٢١).* Border?
		(Weyl. Jackson.)	
439	1217	Elephant advancing to left with uplifted tail: above the elephant the date ٧١٢١ In a double-lined circle with a row of dots.	فرخي ضرب A dotted rosette in the lower part of the field. In a double-lined circle with a row of dots.
		(Weyl.)	
440 M	1218	As on No. 439, but date ٨١٢١ Pl. VIII.	As on No. 439.

* I have not seen this coin and the arrangement of the inscription is conjectural.

8. SALĀMĀBĀD سلام اباد

(The City of Peace.)

This name was applied to the town of Satyamangalam, situated on the Bhavani river, in the northern part of the Coimbatore district. It was a place of considerable military importance during the campaigns of Haidar and Tīpū, because it lies close to the passes through which troops descended to the low country from the Mysore plateau, when operating in the south and towards the west coast. The town had been in the possession of Mysore for about a hundred years before Haidar came into power. It was captured by British troops under Colonel Floyd, in August 1790, but was afterwards abandoned. Satyamangalam remained in the possession of Tīpū up to the time of his death.

A series of roughly executed copper coins was issued from this mint in the years 1216, 1217 and 1218. In all of them, with the exception of a half-paisa of 1216, there is a wide marginal double-lined circle crossed by radiating lines, while in the half-paisa just referred to, the space between the two circles is occupied by three-branched flowers which almost resemble arrow-heads, pointing around the circumference.

The coins of this mint are all more or less rare, the paisas of 1216 and 1217 being perhaps more frequently met with than any of the others, while the quarter and one-eighth paisa are both extremely rare.

SALĀMĀBĀD.

Metal. Number.	Date.	Obverse.	Reverse.
		PAISA.	
Æ 441 M	1216	Elephant advancing to left with uplifted tail: above the tail the date ٦١٢١	اباد سلام ضرب
		In a wide double-lined circle crossed by radiating lines.	On a plain field. In a wide double-lined circle crossed by radiating lines.
442 M	1217	As on No. 441, but date ٧١٢١ and last figure of date to left of the tail.	As on No. 441.
443 M	1218	As on No. 441, but date ٨١٢١ and all the figures to left of the elephant's tail. Pl. VIII.	Do.

SALĀMĀBĀD.

HALF-PAISA.

Metal. Number.	Date.	Obverse.	Reverse.
Æ 444 M	1216	Elephant advancing to left with uplifted tail: above the tail the date ٦١٢١ In a wide double-lined circle crossed by radiating lines.	اباد سلام ضرب On a plain field. In a wide double-lined circle crossed by radiating lines.
445	"	As on No. 444, but date to left of the elephant's tail. In a wide double-lined circle enclosing a flowered pattern. Pl. VIII.	As on No. 444. In a wide double-lined circle enclosing a flowered pattern.
446 M	1217	As on No. 444, but date ٧١٢١ and the last three figures of the date to left of the tail.	As on No. 444.
447 M	1218	As on No. 444, but date ٨١٢١ and all the figures to left of the elephant's tail. Pl. VIII.	Do.

QUARTER-PAISA.

Metal. Number.	Date.	Obverse.	Reverse.
448	1216	Elephant advancing to left with uplifted tail: above the tail the date ٦١٢١ In a wide double-lined circle crossed by radiating lines. Pl. VIII.	اباد سلام ب ضر On a plain field. In a wide double-lined circle crossed by radiating lines.

EIGHTH-PAISA.

Metal. Number.	Date.	Obverse.	Reverse.
449 M	1218	Elephant advancing to left with uplifted tail: the date ٨١٢١ to left of the tail. In a double-lined circle crossed by radiating lines. Pl. VIII.	اباد سلام ب ضر On a plain field. In a double-lined circle crossed by radiating lines.

9. KHĀLIQĀBĀD خالق اباد

(The City of God.)

This fanciful appellation was, we have every reason to believe, given to Dindigul, an important town in the Madura district, with an isolated rock which was formerly strongly fortified rising 280 feet above the surrounding country. It first became included in Mysore territory in 1742, and thirteen years later Haidar Alī was appointed military governor of the place, an appointment which may be said to have been the commencement of his rise to power. Dindigul surrendered to Col. Wood in August 1767, but was retaken by Haidar in the following year. It surrendered once again to Col. Lang in May 1783, and was restored to Tīpū Sultān by the treaty of Mangalore in 1784. It was subsequently taken by Col. Stuart on 22nd August 1790, from which date it ceased to be included in Mysore, and was finally placed under the control of the East India Company by the treaty of 1792. It is on record that Tīpū visited Dindigul in 1788, after founding Farrukhī, but the coinage of Khāliqābād dates from a year earlier than this visit.

Hawkes in 1856 recorded the statement that Khāliqābād was a name given by Tīpū to Chandagāl, near Seringapatam, and this attribution has been followed generally by later writers. In Dr. Taylor's memoir *The Coins of Tīpū Sultān*, issued in 1914, will be found, however, a series of arguments, supplied by the present writer, in favour of identifying the mint with Dindigul rather than Chandagāl, and these may be briefly recapitulated. Chandagāl is an insignificant village at the southern end of the main ford over the River Cauvery to Seringapatam, and is almost within stone throw of the latter place. It is extremely unlikely that Tīpū would locate a second mint so near his chief one, and the places selected for coinage operations were always of importance in some way or other. The coins, which were only in use for a few years, are of coarse execution, and the dies were evidently made by workmen who were ignorant of the characters, which could hardly have been the case in a place close to Seringapatam. Many of the coins are not rare at the present day in the Madura district, and they are certainly commoner there than anywhere else, while of a number of Tīpū's copper coins collected for me at Dindigul some years ago, the majority were of the Khāliqābād mint. In the *History of the Reign of Tīpū Sultān* by Mīr Hussein Alī Khān Kirmānī, it is definitely stated that Khāliqābād was another name for Dindigul, and although Kirmānī is not always correct in his statements, this one may perhaps be accepted. It is in every way likely that such an important fortified town as Dindigul, dominating as it did the northern entrance to the Madura district, would be selected as a fitting location for a mint.

One of the commonest coins of Khāliqābād is a quarter-paisa apparently dated 1225, an impossible year for Dindigul, but as will be seen from the catalogue there are numerous variations of this coin, and I think there can be little doubt that they are the work of Tamil die-cutters who were ignorant of the Arabic numerals, and the year intended was really 1215.

Gold fanams, and copper paisas, half-paisas and quarter-paisas, were struck at Khāliqābād from 1215 to 1218. The last year is recorded by Marsden and Taylor (vide *Coins of Tipū Sultān*, pl. I, fig. 3), but as will be seen from Taylor's figure the last numeral of the date is not erect, and some doubt may in consequence be expressed as to whether the year is not 1217. The coins are all roughly executed and the date is very frequently blundered.

The most usual border is a double-lined circle enclosing oblique lines or dashes, but on some coins the oblique lines are replaced by objects resembling arrow-heads, or Λ- shaped cross-bars.

The gold fanams are now rare, and with the exception of some of the blundered quarter-paisas of 1215 which are not infrequently met with, none of the copper coins can be said to be common. In fact the paisas must be described as moderately rare.

KHĀLIQĀBĀD.

Metal. Number.	Date.	Obverse.	Reverse.
		FANAM.	
AV 450	1215	ح On plain field: in a lined circle with a row of dots.	خالق اباد ١٢١٥ ضرب In a lined circle with a row of dots.
		(British Museum, fide *Jackson.)*	
451 M	1217	As on No. 450. Pl. IX.	As on No. 450, but date ٧١٢١
		PAISA.	
Æ 452	1215	Elephant advancing to left (?) above it the date ٥٩١١ (in error for ٥١٢١) and the word سنه Border?	خالق اباد ضرب Border?
		(British Museum, fide *Jackson.)*	
453 M	1217	Elephant advancing to left with uplifted tail: above the elephant the date ٧١٢١ In a double-lined circle with a row of thick oblique dashes.* Pl. IX.	خالق اباد ضرب On a plain field. In a double-lined circle with a row of thick oblique dashes.

* A Khāliqābād paisa sold at the White-King sale was catalogued as of date 1212. I examined it and found it to be a paisa of 1217.

KHĀLIQĀBĀD.

HALF-PAISA.

Metal. Number.	Date.	Obverse.	Reverse.
Æ 454	1215	Elephant advancing to left with uplifted tail: above the elephant the date ١٢١٥ In a double-lined circle with a row of thick oblique dashes.	خالق اباد ضرب On a plain field. In a double-lined circle with a row of thick oblique dashes.

(Tufnell, pl. IV, 159.)

Metal. Number.	Date.	Obverse.	Reverse.
455 M	1217	As on No. 454, but date <١٢١ Pl. IX.	As on No. 454.
456	1218	As on No. 454 (?), but date ٨١٢١	As on No. 454 (?).

(Marsden.)

QUARTER-PAISA.

Metal. Number.	Date.	Obverse.	Reverse.
457	1215	Elephant advancing to left with uplifted tail: above the elephant the date ١٢٢٥ (in error for ١٢١٥) In a double-lined circle with a row of oblique cross-lines. Pl. IX.	خالق اد ضرب On a plain field. In a double-lined circle with a row of oblique cross-lines.
458	"	As on No. 457, but date ٨٢٢٥ (in error for ١٢١٥)	As on No. 457.
459	"	As on No. 457, but date ٧١٢٥ (in error for ١٢١٥) In a double-lined circle with a row of arrow-heads (ᛉ)	Do. In a double-lined circle with a row of ∧-shaped cross-bars.
460	"	As on No. 457, but date ٢١٦٥ (in error for ١٢١٥) In a double-lined circle with a row of ∧-shaped cross-bars. Pl. IX.	As on No. 459.
461	"	As on No. 457, but date ٦١٢٥ (in error for ١٢١٥)	As on No. 457.

(Weyl.)

Metal. Number.	Date.	Obverse.	Reverse.
		QUARTER-PAISA—*cont.*	
Æ 462	12:5	Elephant advancing to right with uplifted tail: above the elephant the date ٥٢٢١ (in error for ٥١٢١) In a double-lined circle with a row of oblique cross-lines.	As on No. 457.
463	,,	As on No. 462, but date ٥٦٢١ (in error for ٥١٢١)	Do. Pl. IX.
464	,,	As on No. 462, but date ٥٦٦> (in error for ٥١٢١)	Do.
465	1216	As on No. 459, but date ٦١٢١ To the right of the date and separated from it by the tip of the elephant's tail is the numeral ٥	As on No. 459.
		(Jackson, pl. II, 286.)	
466	,,	As on No. 462, but date ٦١٢١	As on No. 457.
		(Jackson.)	
467	,,	As on No. 462, but date ٦١١١ (in error for ٦١٢١) and in a double-lined circle with a row of arrow-heads. Pl. IX.	As on No. 459.
468	1217	As on No. 457, but date < ١٢١ : in a double-lined circle with a row of oblique dashes.	As on No. 457, but in a double-lined circle with a row of oblique dashes.
469	,,	As on No. 468, but date ٧١٢١ : the first two figures separated by the end of the elephant's tail. Pl. IX.	As on No. 468.

KHĀLIQĀBĀD.

Metal. Number.	Date.	Obverse.	Reverse.
		QUARTER-PAISA—*cont.*	
Æ 470	1217	As on No. 469, but in a double-lined circle with a row of arrow-heads.	As on No. 459.
471	,,	As on No. 462, but date ٧١٢١ : in a double-lined circle with a row of arrow-heads. Pl. IX.	Do.
472 M	,,	As on No. 471, but date ٧١١٦ (in error for ٧١٢١)	Do.
473	,,	As on No. 457, but date ٧٦١ (in error probably for ٧١٢١	As on No. 457.
474	,,	As on No. 457, but date ٧١١ (in error probably for ٧١٢١) *(Weyl.)*	Do.
475	1218	As on No. 457, (?), but date ٨١٢١ *(Marsden.)*	Do. (?).
476	—	As on No. 457, but date represented by the figures ٦١ *(Weyl.)*	Do.
477 M	—	As on No. 462, but date represented by the figures ٦٦ : in a double-lined circle with a row of ∧ — shaped cross-bars.	As on No. 459.
478	—	Elephant advancing to left. No date. In a lined circle and ring of dots. *(Jackson.)*	As on No. 468.
479	—	As on No. 478. *(Jackson.)*	خالقم ضرب

10. ZAFARĀBĀD ظفراباد

(The City of Victory.)

This name was at first assigned to Mercara, the capital of Coorg, but in December 1785 (1200 A.H.) it was transferred to Gurramkonda (*vide* Kirkpatrick, pp. 206, 224). From their dates none of the coins could, therefore, have been struck at Mercara.

Gurramkonda, a town in the Cuddapah district with a strong hill-fort, was taken by Haidar Alī in 1768 from the Nawābs of Cuddapah, who owed allegiance to the Nizām. A few years later it surrendered to the Marāthās, from whom, however, it was recaptured by Tīpū Sultān early in 1774. In 1791 the town was invested by British troops and a strong force of the Nizām's, but the fort managed to hold out till the following year, when peace was declared. By the treaty of 1792 the Cuddapah district was restored to the Nizām, by whom in 1800, it along with the Bellary and Anantapūr districts was ceded to the East India Company.

The coins of this mint consist of a small series of paisas and of half and quarter-paisas, struck from 1215 to 1218, but no coin of the year 1217 has yet been recorded. In most of them the border consists of the usual double-lined circle enclosing a row of dots. Two of the half-paisas, however, exhibit peculiar borders; in one of them the double-lined circle on both sides encloses objects resembling arrow-heads, while in the other the border just described occurs on the reverse, and the obverse has groups of three short concentric lines within the double circle.

The least rare of the Zafarābād coins is the half-paisa of 1218, which is still occasionally met with. All the other coins of this mint are more or less rare, and some of them are now very seldom met with.

ZAFARĀBĀD.

Metal. Number.	Date.	Obverse.	Reverse.
		PAISA.	
Æ 480	1216	Elephant advancing to left with uplifted tail: above the elephant the date ١٢١٦ In a double-lined circle with a row of dots.	ظفراباد ضرب On a field ornamented with dotted rosettes. In a double-lined circle with a row of dots.

(Schulman: White-King Catalogue. Jackson.)

ZAFARĀBĀD.

Metal. Number.	Date.	Obverse.	Reverse.
		PAISA—*cont.*	
Æ 481	1218	As on No. 480, but date ٨١٢١	As on No. 480.
		(Tufnell, pl. IV, 191.)	
482 M	”	As on No. 481, but date ٨١٩١ (in error for ٨١٢١)	Do. Pl. IX.
		HALF-PAISA.	
483	1215	Elephant advancing to right with uplifted tail : above the elephant the date ٥١٢١ In a double-lined circle enclosing objects resembling arrow-heads.	ظفراباد ضرب On a field ornamented with dotted rosettes. In a double-lined circle enclosing objects resembling arrow-heads.
484 M	1216	Elephant advancing to left with uplifted tail : above the elephant the date ٦١٢١ In a double-lined circle enclosing groups of three short concentric lines.	As on No. 483, but the field plain. In a double-lined circle crossed by irregular lines which in parts tend to resemble arrow-heads. Pl. IX.
485 M	”	As on No. 484. In a double-lined circle with a row of dots. Pl. IX.	As on No. 483. In a double-lined circle with a row of dots.
486 M	1218	As on No. 485, but date ٨١٢١	As on No. 485.
		QUARTER-PAISA.	
487	1218	Elephant advancing to left with uplifted tail : above the elephant the date ٨١٢١ In a double-lined circle with a row of dots.	ظفراباد ضرب In a double-lined circle with a row of dots.

11. DHĀRWĀR دهاروار

KHWURSHED-SAWĀD خورشید سواد

(The sun-blackened place.)

From Dhārwār, the chief town of the district of the same name in the extreme south of the Bombay Presidency, were issued in the year 1216 two coins in gold and one in silver. In the two following years a limited number of coins in gold, silver and copper, were struck at the same mint, to which the fanciful name Khwurshed-sawād was now applied. This strongly fortified town was taken by Haidar Alī from the Marāthās in 1778, the garrison of the fort being deceived by an ingenious stratagem. It finally surrendered to the combined British and Marāthā army on 7th April 1791, after a siege of twenty-nine weeks. By the treaty of Seringapatam it was, in the following year, restored to the Marāthās.

The pagoda with the mint name Dhārwār follows the earlier or sultānī type, while the two later pagodas, in which the mint appears as Khwurshed-sawād, conform to the fārūqī type; in all three the border consists of a lined circle enclosing a row of dots, but in the two later coins and on the reverse of the oldest one the circle appears to be single. The rupees also bear the two mint names; all belong to the later type or imāmī, and the border is a single or double-lined circle enclosing a row of dots. Only three copper coins are known, and these have a distinctive border consisting of a wide double-lined circle enclosing dots in groups of three, arranged in triangular fashion, with considerable intervals between. Two peculiar 'arrow-head' marks are noticeable on the reverse of the paisa of 1217.

The coins of this mint are all more or less rare, the paisa of 1218 being perhaps the least rare. The rupees are of considerable rarity, and the same may also be said of the half-paisa.

DHĀRWĀR.

Metal. Number.	Date.	Obverse.	Reverse.
		PAGODA.	
AV 488 M	1216	ح دهاروار On a granulated field: in a double-lined circle with a row of dots. Pl. IX.	هو محمد السلطان العــا ٦١٢١ دل منه In a single-lined circle with a row of dots.

DHĀRWĀR.
KHWURSHED-SAWĀD.

Metal. Number.	Date.	Obverse.	Reverse.

FANAM.

Metal. Number.	Date.	Obverse.	Reverse.
AI 489	1216	ح On a plain field: in a lined circle with a row of dots.	٦١٢١ دهاروار ضرب In a lined circle with a row of dots.*

(Schulman: White-King Catalogue.)

RUPEE.

Metal. Number.	Date.	Obverse.	Reverse.
AR 490	1216	محمد احمد دین درجهان است ح ضرب روشن زفتح حیدر امام ٦١٢١ دهاروار سال مارا سنه In a double-lined circle with a row of dots.	هو الو السلطان حیدر تاریخ سال مع العادل جلوس میوم بهاري سنه ٦ جلو In a double-lined circle with a row of dots.

(Jackson, pl. II, 288.)

PAGODA.

Metal. Number.	Date.	Obverse.	Reverse.
AI 491 M	1217	فاروقح شهید خور سواد ٧ سنه The ح (Haidar's initial) is united to the last letter of fārūqī. In a lined circle with a row of dots. Pl. IX.	هو محمد لسلطان حیدر ٧١٢١ الو العادل سنه A few dotted rosettes in the field. In a lined circle with a row of dots.
492	1218	As on No. 491, but regnal year ٨	As on No. 491, but date ٨١٢١

* I have not seen this coin and the inscription on the reverse is conjectural.

KHWURSHED-SAWĀD.

Metal. Number	Date.	Obverse.	Reverse.
		RUPEE.	
AR 493	1217	محمد احمد دين در جهان است ح ضرب روشن زفتح حيدر امام شيد سواد سال سراب خور منه ١٢١٧ In a lined circle with a row of dots.	هو الو السلطان حيد تاريخ سال مع العادل جلوس س ميمنت بهاري منه ٧ جلو A dotted rosette near the upper margin. In a lined circle with a row of dots.
494	1218	As on No. 493, but cyclic year شتا and date ١٢١٨	As on No. 493, but regnal year ٨
		PAISA.	
Æ 495	1217	Elephant advancing to left with uplifted tail: above the tail the date ١٢١٧ In a wide double-lined circle with groups of three dots ∴ placed at considerable intervals.	سواد شيد خورب ضر A mark resembling an arrow-head near the upper margin, and a second smaller one between the two upper lines of the inscription. The same border as on the obverse.
		A variety of this coin in the British Museum has a series of dotted rosettes on the obverse above the elephant.	
496 M	1218	As on No. 495, but date ١٢١٨ Pl. IX.	As on No. 495, but without the arrow-head marks.

KHWURSHED-SAWĀD.

HALF-PAISA.

Metal. Number.	Date.	Obverse.	Reverse.
Æ 497 M	1217	Elephant advancing to left with uplifted tail: above the elephant three groups of four-dotted rosettes and the date ١٢١٧ In a wide double-lined circle, with groups of three dots ∴ placed at considerable intervals. Pl. IX.	سواد شــيد خور ضرب On a field ornamented with dotted rosettes. The same border as on the obverse.

12. NAZARBĀR نظر بار

(Scattering favour.)

In 1787, Tīpū Sultān wishing to destroy the evidences of Hindu power, demolished the old fort and town of Mysore, and erected a new fort about a mile to the east of the older one, to which the above fanciful name was given. Mysore or Mahishūr derives its name from Mahishāsura, the buffalo-headed monster destroyed by Kāli, who is locally known as Chāmundi. It has been the capital of the State since the death of Tīpū, but it was an important city, and the seat of the Rājās or Wodeyars, long before the Muhammadan usurpation. The fort of Nazarbīr was still unfinished in 1799, and the stones used in its construction, which had actually been taken from the old fort, were brought back and used in the restoration of the latter.

The coinage of this mint is limited to a paisa, half-paisa and quarter-paisa, struck in 1216, all of which are somewhat rare, the half-paisa being, however, more frequently met with than the other two. The border in all is a double-lined circle enclosing a row of dots, as in the Seringapatam coins. Mysore is only a few miles distant from Seringapatam, where possibly the Nazarbār coins were actually struck.

NAZARBĀR.

Metal.	Number.	Date.	Obverse.	Reverse.
			PAISA.	
Æ	498 M	1216	Elephant advancing to left with uplifted tail: above the tail the date ٦١٢١ In a double-lined circle with a row of dots. Pl. IX.	نظر بار ضرب On a field ornamented with dotted rosettes. In a double-lined circle with a row of dots.
			HALF-PAISA.	
	499 M	1216	As on No. 498. Pl. IX.	As on No. 498.
			QUARTER-PAISA.	
	500	1216	As on No. 498.	As on No. 498.

BIBLIOGRAPHY.

The following books or publications, which deal directly or indirectly with the coins of Haidar Alī and Tīpū Sultān, are arranged in chronological order :—

I. A Narrative of the Operations of Captain Little's Detachment and of the Mahratta Army, commanded by Purseram Bhow; during the late Confederacy in India, against the Nawab Tippoo Sultan Bahadur. By Edward Moor, Lieutenant on the Bombay Establishment. London: 1794.

Coins of Tīpū Sultān on pp. 465–481. Plates I and II.

II. View of the Origin and Conduct of the War with Tippoo Sultaun. By Lieut.-Col. A. Beatson. London: 1800.

III. Select Letters of Tippoo Sultan. By William Kirkpatrick. London: 1811.

IV. Numismata Orientalia Illustrata. The Oriental Coins, ancient and modern, of his Collection, described and historically illustrated. By William Marsden, F.R.S. Part II. London: 1825.

Coins of Tīpū Sultān on pp. 699–725. Plates XLV, XLVI.

V. A brief sketch of the Gold, Silver, and Copper Coinage of Mysore. By Lieut. H. P. Hawkes. Bangalore: 1856.

Coins of Haidar Alī and Tīpū Sultān on pp. 1–12. Plates I and II.

VI. Beschreibung der bekanntesten Kupfermünzen von Josef Neumann. Dritter Band. Prag: 1863.

Coins of Tīpū Sultān on pp. 48–53. Plates XLIV, XLV, XLVII.

A few references also in Sechster Band: 1872, p. 160. Plate 79.

VII. History of the Reign of Tīpū Sultān. By Mir Hussein Ali Khan Kirmani. Translated by Col. W. Miles. London: 1864.

Names of forts on p. 83; reference to coins p. 285.

VIII. Verzeichniss von Münzen und Denkmünzen der Jules Fonrobert'schen Sammlung. Gefertigt von Adolph Weyl. Berlin: 1878.

Coins of Haidar Alī and Tīpū Sultān, pp. 229–236.

IX. Government Central Museum, Madras. Coins. Catalogue No. 1. Mysore. By Edgar Thurston. Madras: 1888.

Coins of Haidar Alī and Tīpū Sultān, pp. 9–14, 19–28 and 34–44. Plates I to III and V to X.

X. Catalogue of Mysore Coins in the Collection of the Government Museum, Bangalore. By Capt. R. H. Campbell Tufnell. Madras: 1889.

Coins of Haidar Alī and Tīpū Sultān, pp. 7–14, 22–52. Plates I to IV.

XI. The Names of the Coins of Tipu Sultan. By E. Hultzsch, Ph. D. Indian Antiquary, Vol. XVIII, p. 315, 1889.

XII. Mysore—A Gazetteer. By B. Lewis Rice. Volume I. London: 1897.

Coins of Haidar Alī and Tīpū Sultān, pp. 803–807. Plate II.

XIII. Catalogue Collection du Dr. L. White King, venté à Amsterdam le 18 Décembre 1905 et jours suivants. J. Schulman. Quatrième Partie. Amsterdam: 1905.

Coins of Haidar Alī and Tīpū Sultān, p. 6, Pl. I.

XIV. Coin Collecting in Mysore. By Major R. P. Jackson. British Numismatic Journal, Vol. V, 1909.

Coins of Haidar Alī and Tīpū Sultān, pp. 13–45 (separate copy). Plates I and II

XV. Report of the Mysore Archæological Department for the year 1912-13. By R. Narasimhachar.

Coins of Tīpū Sultān on Pl. IX. There are short references to Tīpū's coins in some of the other Reports of this series.

XVI. The Coins of Tīpū Sultān. (Occasional Memoirs of the Numismatic Society of India). By Rev. G. P. Taylor, M.A., D.D. Oxford: 1914. Two plates.

XVII. Note on the Dates of the Maulūdī Era of Tīpū Sultān of Mysore. By J. R. Henderson. Numismatic Supplement No. XXIII, p. 251, Journal Asiatic Society of Bengal (New Series), Vol. X, 1914.

LIST OF COINS ILLUSTRATED

The numbers of the gold and silver coins are followed by the usual letters for these metals, while the copper coins are merely numbered. In all cases the numbers are those under which the coins are described in the catalogue.

PLATE I.

Coins of Haidar Alī and Tīpū Sultān (Seringapatam).

1. Haidar Alī.—Pagoda (Siva and Parvatī).
3. " " (Muhammad Shāh); Gooty, 1194.
5. " Half-pagoda (Siva and Parvatī).
6. " " (Vishnu).
7. " Fanam (Siva and Parvatī).
8. " " 1189.
10. " " 1166 (?).
11. " Paisa; Seringapatam, 1195.
13. " " Bellary.
14. " " Bellary.
15. " " Seringapatam.
17. " Double-cash, with Kanarese numerals.
22. " Tiger and battle-axe; half-paisa.
23. " " quarter-paisa.
25. " " eighth-paisa.
3. Tīpū Sultān.—Seringapatam. Ahmadī, 1215.
8. " " Sadīqī, 1217.
13. " " Pagoda, 1198.
14. " " " 1200.
17. " " " (fārūqī), 1217.
23. " " Fanam, 1197.
41. " " Double-rupee, 1198.
46. " " " 1216.

NOTE.—The coins of Haidar Alī occupy the upper half and those of Tīpū Sultān the lower half of the plate. As the two series are numbered separately in the catalogue similar numbers occur in the two parts of the plate.

PLATE II.

Coins of Tīpū Sultān (Seringapatam)—*cont.*

47. Seringapatam.—Double-rupee (haidarī), 1216.
53. " Rupee (imāmī), 1216.
57. " " 1219.
67. " Half-rupee (ābidī), 1222.
70. " Quarter-rupee (bāqirī), 1217.
77. " Eighth-rupee (jafarī), 1221.
83. " Sixteenth-rupee (kāzimī), 1221.
92. " Double-paisa (othmānī), 1218.
93. " " 1218.
98. " Double-paisa (mushtarī), 1221.
99. " " 1222.

PLATE III.

Coins of Tīpū Sultān (Seringapatam)—*cont.*

101. Seringapatam.—Double-paisa (mushtarī), 1224.
107. „ Paisa, 1201.
118. „ „ 1220; 1260 in error.
119. „ „ 1221.
120. „ „ 1221.
121. „ „ (zohrā), 1221.
122. „ „ (zohra), 1221.
133-a. „ „ (zohra), 1224; variety with 7-dotted rosette.
133-c. „ „ (zohra), 1224; variety with star.
133-d. „ „ „ variety with pointed mark.
140. „ Half-paisa, 1201.
141. „ „ 1215.
142. „ „ 1215.
148. „ „ 1220.
151. „ „ (bahrām), 1221.

PLATE IV.

Coins of Tīpū Sultān (Seringapatam—*cont.* Nagar).

157. Seringapatam.—Half-paisa (bahrām), 1223.
159. „ „ 1224.
161. „ „ 1226.
162. „ Half-paisa, no date.
165. „ Quarter-paisa, 1200.
166. „ „ 1201.
175. „ „ 1221.
176. „ „ 1221.
180. „ „ (akhtar), 1222.
183. „ „ „ 1223.
184. „ „ „ 1223.
186. „ „ „ 1225.
187. „ „ „ 1226.
188. „ „ no date.
191. „ Eighth-paisa, 1218.
194. „ „ (qutb), 1222.
195. „ „ „ 1224.
200. Nagar.—Pagoda, 1198.
204. „ „ (fārūqī), 1216.
207. „ Fanam, 1198.
214. „ „ 1220.
219. „ Rupee (imāmī), 1216.
221. „ Double-paisa (othmānī), 1218.
223. „ „ (mushtarī), 1223.

PLATE V.

Coins of Tīpū Sultān (Nagar—*cont.*).

224. Nagar.—Double-paisa (mushtarī), 1224.
226. „ „ 1226.
228. „ Paisa, 1197.
228-a. „ „ 1197; rosette variety.
230. „ „ 1200.

235. Nagar.—Paisa, 1217.
242. „ „ (zohrā), 1222.
249. „ „ „ 1224.
251. „ „ „ 1225; 216 in error on the obverse.
252. „ „ „ 1225; 1223 in error on the obverse.
255. „ „ 1226 (?); 216 in error.
259. „ Half-paisa, 1200.
265. „ „ (bahrām), 1222.

PLATE VI.

Coins of Tīpū Sultān (Nagar—*cont.* Gooty).

270. Nagar.—Half-paisa (bahrām), 1227.
272. „ Quarter-paisa, 1198.
275. „ Quarter-paisa, 1216.
282. „ Quarter-paisa (akhtar), 1226.
283. „ Quarter-paisa (zohrā in error for akhtar), 1226.
285. „ Eighth-paisa (qutb), 1226.
286. Gooty.—Paisa, 1215.
287. „ Paisa, 1216.
291. „ Paisa, 1218.
295. „ Paisa, 1221; 1661 in error.
297. „ Paisa, 1222.
299. „ Paisa (zohra), 1224.
301. „ Paisa (zohra), 1225; 1663 in error on the obverse.
310. „ Half-paisa, 1218.
312. „ Half-paisa, 1222.
315. „ Half-paisa (bahrām), 1224.
316. „ Half-paisa (bahrām), 1225; 1665 in error on the reverse.
317. „ Half-paisa (bahrām), 1225; 1663 in error on the obverse, and 166 (3) in error on the reverse.
318. „ Half-paisa (bahrām), 1226; 1222 in error on the obverse.
322. „ Quarter-paisa, 1216.
331. „ Quarter-paisa, 1223; 1663 in error on the obverse.
331-a. „ Quarter-paisa, 1223; as the last coin, but the tail of the elephant depressed.
332. „ Quarter-paisa, 1223; 1663 (with reversed 3) on the obverse.

PLATE VII.

Coins of Tīpū Sultān (Gooty—*cont.* Bangalore, Chitaldrūg, Calicut).

336. Gooty.—Quarter-paisa (bahrām in error for akhtar), 1225; 1222 in error on the reverse.
338. „ Quarter-paisa (bahrām in error for akhtar), 1225; 1665 in error on the reverse.
342. „ Quarter-paisa (akhtar), 1226.
345. „ Quarter-paisa (akhtar), 1226; 1222 in error on the obverse.
356. Bangalore.—Paisa, 1216.
358. „ Paisa, 1217.
362. „ Half-paisa, 1215.
364. „ Half-paisa, 1216.

368. Bangalore.—Half-paisa, 1218.
379. „ Quarter-paisa, 1218.
383. „ Eighth-paisa, 1218.
385. Chitaldrūg.—Double-paisa (othmānī), 1218.
389. „ Paisa, 1215.
393. „ Paisa, 1216.
394. „ Paisa, 1216; larger and thinner variety.
398. „ Half-paisa, 1215.
400. „ Half-paisa, 1217.
404. „ Quarter-paisa, 1217.
409. Calicut.—Fanam, 1199.
412. „ Fanam, 1215.
415. „ Paisa, 1198.
417. „ Paisa, 1200.

PLATE VIII.

Coins of Tīpū Sultān (Calicut—*cont.* Feroke, Satyamangalam).

416. Calicut.—Paisa, 1199.
418. „ Paisa, 1200; fourth regnal year.
420. „ Paisa, 1215; fourth regnal year.
421. „ Paisa, 1215.
422. „ Paisa, no date.
423. „ Quarter-paisa, no date.
424. „ Quarter-paisa, no date.
426. Feroke.—Fanam, 1216.
429. „ Double-paisa (othmānī), 1218.
434. „ Paisa, 1218.
436. „ Half-paisa, 1217.
440. „ Quarter-paisa, 1218.
443. Satyamangalam.—Paisa, 1218.
445. „ Half-paisa, 1216.
447. „ Half-paisa, 1218.
448. „ Quarter-paisa, 1216.
449. „ Eighth-paisa, 1218.

PLATE IX.

Coins of Tīpū Sultān (Dindigul, Gurramkonda, Dhārwār, Mysore).

451. Dindigul.—Fanam, 1217.
453. „ Paisa, 1217.
455. „ Half-paisa, 1217.
457. „ Quarter-paisa, 1215; 1225 in error.
460. „ Quarter-paisa, 1215; 2165 in error.
463. „ Quarter-paisa, 1215; 1665 in error.
466. „ Quarter-paisa, 1216; 1116 in error.
468. „ Quarter-paisa, 1217.
471. „ Quarter-paisa, 1217.
482. Gurramkonda.—Paisa, 1218; 1618 in error.
484. „ Half-paisa, 1216.
485. „ Half-paisa, 1216.
488. Dhārwār.—Pagoda, 1216.
491. „ Pagoda (fārūqī), 1217.
496. „ Paisa, 1218.
497. „ Half-paisa, 1217.
498. Mysore.—Paisa, 1216.
499. „ Half-paisa, 1216.

ERRATA.

Plate I. *For* 23 AV *read* 25 AV.

Plate IV. The obverse and reverse of 204 AV have been transposed.

Plate VI. No. 331 shows a variety in which the elephant's tail is raised. No. 331-*a* shows the tail depressed as described in the Catalogue.

Plate VII. *For* 389 *read* 391.

" No. 409 AV shows a variety in which the last letter of the mint-name is omitted.

Plate IX. *For* 466 *read* 467.

" *For* 468 *read* 469.

" The obverse and reverse of 488 AV and 491 AV have been transposed.

PLATE I

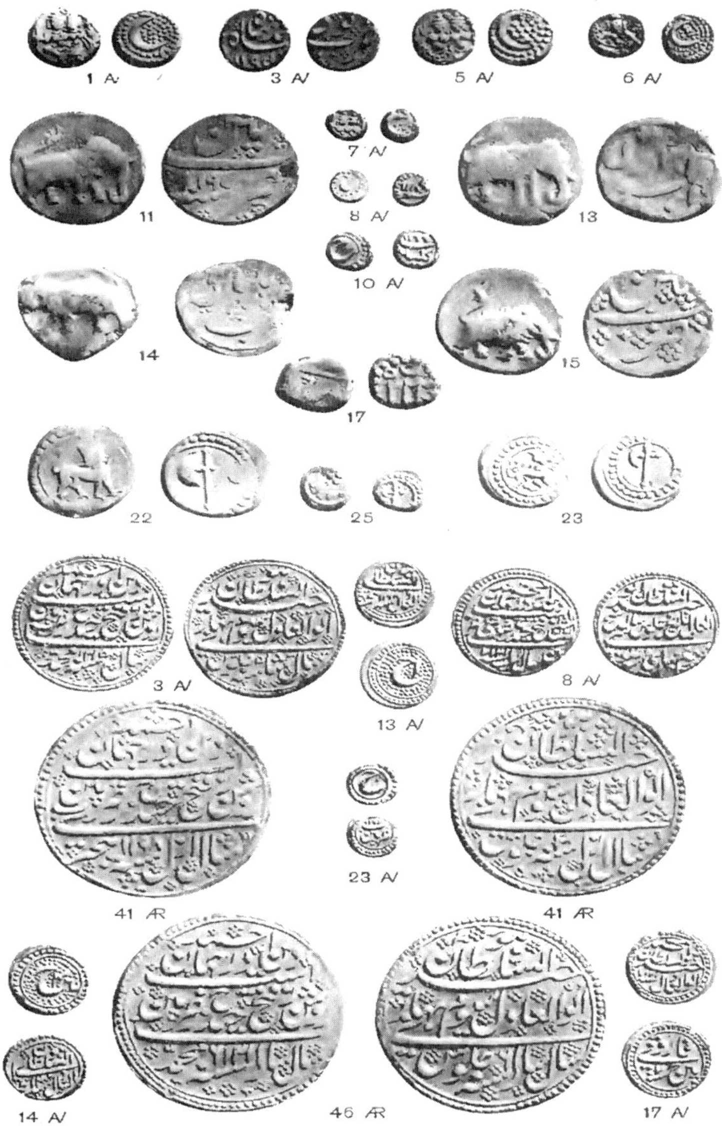

HAIDAR ALĪ—TĪPŪ SULTĀN; SERINGAPATAM

PLATE II

TIPŪ SULTĀN; SERINGAPATAM

101 101 107 118 119 120 121 122 133 a 133 c 133 d 140 141 142 148 151

TĪPŪ SULTAN; SERINGAPATAM

PLATE IV

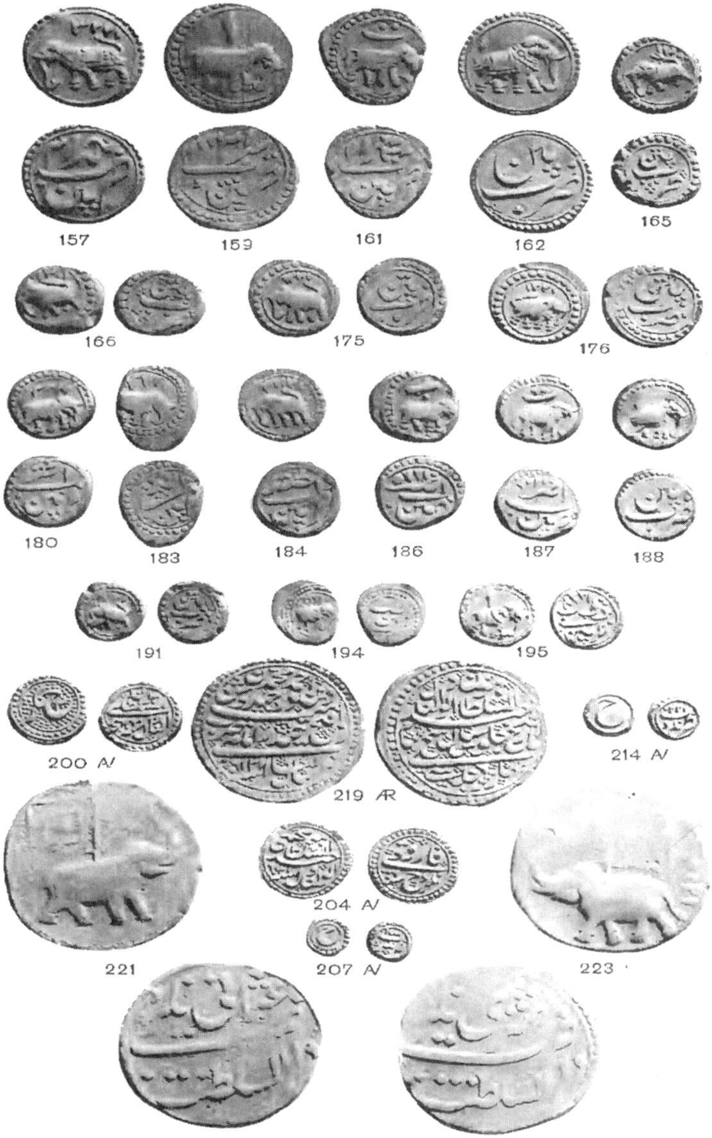

TĪPU SULTĀN; SERINGAPATAM, NAGAR

PLATE V

224

226

228

228 a

230

235

242

249

251

252

255

259

265

TĪPŪ SULTĀN; NAGAR

PLATE VI

TĪPŪ SULTĀN; NAGAR, GOOTY

PLATE VII

TĪPŪ SULTĀN; GOOTY, BANGALORE, CHITALDRŪG, CALICUT

PLATE VIII

TĪPŪ SULTĀN; CALICUT, FEROKE, SATYAMANGALAM

TĪPŪ SULTĀN; DINDIGUL, GURRAMKONDA, DHĀRWĀR, MYSORE